D0469327

Business Finance
for the
Numerically Challenged

By
The Editors of Career Press

Business Finance

for the

Numerically Challenged

By
The Editors of Career Press

CAREER PRESS
3 Tice Road
P.O. Box 687
Franklin Lakes, NJ 07417
1-800-CAREER-1
201-848-0310 (NJ and outside U.S.)
Fax: 201-848-1727

Copyright © 1998 by Career Press, Inc.

All rights reserved under the Pan-American and International Copyright Conventions. This book may not be reproduced, in whole or in part, in any form or by any means electronic or mechanical, including photocopying, recording, or by any information storage and retrieval system now known or hereafter invented, without written permission from the publisher, The Career Press.

BUSINESS FINANCE FOR THE NUMERICALLY CHALLENGED
ISBN 1-56414-314-7 $11.99
Cover design by Foster & Foster
Printed in the U.S.A. by Book-mart Press

To order this title by mail, please include price as noted above, $2.50 handling per order, and $1.50 for each book ordered. Send to: Career Press, Inc., 3 Tice Road, P.O. Box 687, Franklin Lakes, NJ 07417.

Or call toll-free 1-800-CAREER-1 (in NJ and Canada: 201-848-0310) to order using VISA or MasterCard, or for further information on books from Career Press.

Library of Congress Cataloging-in-Publication Data

Business finance for the numerically challenged / by the editors of Career Press.
    p.   cm.
    Includes index.
    ISBN 1-56414-314-7 (pbk.)
    1. Business enterprises--Finance.   2. Financial statements.
    3. Business mathematics.   I. Career Press Inc.
    HG4026.B87   1998   97-37337
    658. 15--dc21   CIP

Acknowledgments

This book is the result of the commitment of many individuals who together focused on the goal of creating a business finance book that explains the subject in unpretentious terms. More than anyone, though, this book could not have been written without the skills and expertise of our resident math and finance whiz, Ian Mahaney.

We'd like to thank Ian for devoting his time to writing a book that will be an asset for businesspeople and others who need to brush up on math and financial skills. For those of us who worked on this project with Ian, we can say that finance is a subject easily learned!

Contents

Finance Is Easy to Learn

Most people who were never finance or economics majors in college (which is the majority of us) can't address the challenge of learning business finance without the sarcastic, "Finance, it would take me years to learn that. Besides, the accounting department takes care of that!" But finance isn't that difficult to learn. In fact, it's a subject where the basics can be mastered fairly easily. Four chapters of *Business Finance for the Numerically Challenged* will do just that. You'll learn the elements of business finance, such as the purpose of a balance sheet, how it relates to the cash that flows through a firm, and how to budget the firm based on cash flow.

Chapter 1 addresses math, an essential factor when dealing with the accounting or sales of any firm. The math review presents necessary math that you probably learned long ago, but have since forgotten during the many years when calculators have been around. Calculators are a great means to an end when used properly, but your knowledge of basic math can never be replaced by a machine. These basic math skills that will be developed can be applied to many fields and will be applied to the financial reporting that follows in Chapters 2 through 5.

The second chapter helps to explain the basis of business finance through the use of basic financial statements: the balance sheet, income statement, and cash flow statement. The chapter will teach you invaluable terms, definitions, and each statement's importance in regard to the basic elements of finance.

Chapter 3 applies the knowledge of financial statements outlined in Chapter 2 to analyze a firm's performance, answering questions such as, "Is this firm performing up to its capabilities?" Or more specifically, "Is it using assets to its potential?"

Forecasting the firm's economic tendencies is discussed in Chapter 4. This will acquaint you with projecting the future—a huge asset in that you will be able to predict trends in order to take advantage of financially good times and to avoid the pitfalls of economic weakness.

Concluding is a brief chapter on budgeting, demonstrating how to prepare and read a budget and understand its benefits.

A complete understanding of the basic structure of finance is taught without any confusing economic terms or references to Dun & Bradstreet. The basics of finance taught here will not provide you with the knowledge to land a job in the financial division of a large corporate bank, but it will increase your ability to understand business finance and complement your understanding of a specific business.

Chapter 1

The Essential Math Review

Business finance is based on math, and it is essential to develop basic math skills if you want to understand finance. Basic math skills will help you read financial statements, analyze them, and communicate the results to co-workers with more success. In other words, the finance you want to learn will be enhanced by the math you need to know.

The math review that follows will refresh the basic skills you learned in the past but may have forgotten. If you feel that you are comfortable with arithmetic, you can skip to Chapter 2 and begin learning about financial statements. After you've read this chapter, if you still feel uneasy about your math skills, another book in this series, *Business Math for the Numerically Challenged*, may be useful to you. It provides a more in-depth review of the basic math topics discussed here and analyzes other related topics and applications.

Grammar school and high school taught us that the base-10 system is the foundation of mathematics. Every number is categorized by and comprises a value and digits. The value of a number is the total it represents, and each digit—the tens, ones, tenths, hundredths, etc.—has a value within it, ranging from 0 to 9, and embodies the total value of the number.

Addition

Addition is the combination of two numbers—one number is joined with another number to produce a third, usually larger, number. The number line represents addition quite well. If a number, say 6, is to be added to another number, say 7, we write 7 + 6. This represents the movement of six whole numbers to the right of 7 on the number line, totaling 13. Thirteen is the sum of 7 and (+) 6 and can be written as follows:

$$7 + 6 = 13 \qquad \textbf{or} \qquad \begin{array}{r} 7 \\ +6 \\ \hline 13 \end{array}$$

7 + 6 is simple addition. In actuality, addition of any numbers consisting of more than one digit is an application of simple addition, which we complete by adding one digit at a time. The following example highlights this practice.

$$\begin{array}{r} \$1,584.76 \\ + \quad \$786.48 \\ \hline \end{array}$$

The progression is to add the smallest digits—the hundredths—first, and the largest—the thousands—last. Add the hundredths digits (the digit all the way on the right in this example): 6 + 8 = 14 hundredths, and because 14 is greater than 9 (14>9),we need to carry the tenths value because this sum is too large to be contained in a single digit. The digit to be carried to the next column—the tenths place in this case—is 1 tenth (or 10 hundredths) and is carried by superscripting 1 above the tenths column. Four hundredths remain that were not carried because 4 is a number that fits into the hundredths digit.

$$
\begin{array}{r}
1 \\
\$1,584.76 \\
+ \quad \$786.48 \\
\hline
4
\end{array}
$$

Next, we add the tenths digits and so forth to the thousands digit, carrying any necessary numbers along the way to result in:

$$
\begin{array}{r}
1\ 1\ 1\ 1\ \ 1 \\
\$1,584.76 \\
+ \quad \$786.48 \\
\hline
\$2,371.24
\end{array}
$$

If you had trouble adding without the solution drawn in detail, use the following notes in adding each digit:

- *Tenths:* $1 + 7 + 4 = 12$
- *Ones:* $1 + 4 + 6 = 11$
- *Tens:* $1 + 8 + 8 = 17$
- *Hundreds:* $1 + 5 + 7 = 13$
- *Thousands:* $1 + 1 = 2$

Here is a step-by-step demonstration of the addition process.

Example: $789,600.89
        + $ 589.71
----

a.
```
        1
   $789,600.89
 + $     589.71
             0
```

b.
```
       1 1
   $789,600.89
 + $     589.71
            60
```

c.
```
      1 1 1
   $789,600.89
 + $     589.71
          0.60
```

d.
```
      1 1 1
   $789,600.89
 + $     589.71
         90.60
```

e.
```
     1   11 1
   $789,600.89
 + $     589.71
        190.60
```

f.
```
     11  11 1
   $789,600.89
 + $     589.71
      0,190.60
```

g.
```
     11  11 1
   $789,600.89
 + $     589.71
   $790,190.60
```

The following are exercises to help you with your addition skills. The previous example was completed step-by-step, so keep in mind that you can and should use any shortcuts possible to reduce the time needed to add. If you find that you can add two steps together without being confused, add two steps together. If three steps is your limit, take three at a time. If you find that estimating the results will help you to find results quickly and you don't need an exact figure, then by all means, estimate. The point is that in math, as long as you can come up with the right answer, the steps you take to get there can vary. So use what works for you.

The final piece of advice is to use a calculator if you need quick results. If you find that you understand addition skills (or other skills for that matter) and a calculator will quicken your results, use one. You make mistakes; I make mistakes; Newton, though he never liked to admit it, made mistakes; Einstein too. But a calculator (if used properly) is never wrong.

Now try your hand at the following. The answers follow.

1. $4,780
    + $ 209

6. $22,741.28
    + $ 7,393.36

2. $523.80
    + $472.19

7. 455,377
    + 812,906

3. $5,288
    + $2,215

8. 361,920.772
    + 39,087.325

4. $8,897.56
    + $3,469.34

9. 1,257,982
    + 679,365

5. $4,937.44
    + $7,578.58

10. 490,239.310
    + 67,543.099

- -

Answers:

1. $4,989
2. $995.99
3. $7,503
4. $12,366.90
5. $12,516.02

6. $30,134.64
7. 1,268,283
8. 401,008.097
9. 1,937,347
10. 557,782.409

Subtraction

Subtraction, like addition, can be represented by movement on the number line. The process of subtracting a number, 5 for instance, from another number, say 9, involves removing the value of 5 from the value of 9, or moving 5 whole numbers to the left of 9 on the number line. Removing 5 from 9 can be written as follows:

$$9 - 5 = 4 \quad \textbf{or} \quad \begin{array}{r} 9 \\ -\ 5 \\ \hline 4 \end{array}$$

Again, like addition, subtracting numbers with two or more digits is an application of simple subtraction. The following example portrays this application.

At 10:30, you return with the expense report in hand. While displaying the smile that you can tell expresses how impressed he is with himself, your boss unfolds the phone bill on your desk and figures, probably from the chat rooms, that expenses are high because of the phone bill. His search through the bill reveals your phone line has charges of $605.89. He suspects that the total of the other lines will give him a better indication of the phone bill. He asks you to find that total, and present it to him. You are very capable in the ways of addition and even wiser in the relationships of numbers. You know that subtraction reverses the *process of addition, or represents movement to the left on the number line. Instead of adding the other lines together, subtract your phone line from the total phone bill to conclude the sum of the other lines:*

$$\begin{array}{r} \$1{,}584.76 \\ - \ \$605.89 \end{array}$$

To illustrate subtraction of complex numbers such as these, it's best to arrange each digit in its corresponding place value (according to the base ten system):

1 thousand	5 hundreds	8 tens	4 ones	7 tenths	6 hundredths
−	6 hundreds	0 tens	5 ones	8 tenths	9 hundredths

Seven dimes and 6 pennies is the same amount of money as 6 dimes and 16 pennies. It may look different, but it represents the same total value. In numeric terms, the tenths digit is the equivalent of the dimes digit and the hundredths digit is the equivalent of the pennies. Therefore, we can say that 7 tenths and 6 hundredths has the same value as 6 tenths and 16 hundredths. The same is true for any digits. This is the premise we will use to subtract in the problem now being illustrated.

Eight tens and 4 ones hold the same value as 7 tens and 14 ones. These values are transferable in any arithmetic problem, but extremely useful in subtraction problems when one of the digits of the minuend (the number that is being subtracted from) holds less value than the corresponding digit of the subtrahend (the number that is being subtracted.) This is useful because we can "borrow" value from a larger digit in order to make the top digit larger than the bottom digit. The final result of a problem must be delivered with each digit valued from 0 to 9, but it is acceptable during the course of the problem to change the composition of a number to suit single subtraction.

Because 6 hundredths (top) is less than 9 hundredths (bottom) in the hundredths digit, it is impossible to subtract 9 from 6 without resulting in a negative number, so we rewrite $1,584.76 in the problem to incorporate the fact that 76 cents can be 6 tenths and 16 hundredths instead of 7 tenths and 6 hundredths, and subtract the hundredths:

1 thousand	5 hundreds	8 tens	4 ones	6 tenths	16 hundredths
−	6 hundreds	0 tens	5 ones	8 tenths	9 hundredths

The remaining digits are subtracted in the same method. If the subtrahend (the bottom digit) is greater than the minuend (the top digit), then borrow from the next largest digit so that the minuend is greater than the subtrahend. An explanation of each digit explains the solution.

$0 thousand	15 hundreds	7 tens	13 ones	16 tenths	16 hundredths
—	6 hundreds	0 tens	5 ones	8 tenths	9 hundredths
	9 hundreds	7 tens	8 ones	8 tenths	7 hundredths

If you had trouble subtracting, use these notes as a guide:

- *Tenths:* By borrowing from the ones column, $6 - 8$ becomes $16 - 8 = 8$.

- *Ones:* Borrowing 1 ten (or 10 ones) from the tens digit gives you the simple subtraction, $13 - 5 = 8$.

- *Tens:* $7 - 0 = 7$.

- *Hundreds:* By borrowing 1 from the thousands, the hundreds subtraction transforms to $15 - 6 = 9$.

or

$$\begin{array}{r} \$1,584.76 \\ - \underline{\$605.89} \\ \$978.87 \end{array}$$

or

$$\$1,584.76 - \$605.89 = \$978.87$$

The long method of subtraction that was just exemplified outlines a method that can be used to subtract, but is quite tedious.

Try some of the following problems using the long method to become comfortable with it before proceeding.

1.	567 − 365	7.	987,678 − 42,779
2.	109.9 − 103.6	8.	87.50 − 69.59
3.	42 − 35	9.	1,298 − 312
4.	67.67 − 56.76	10.	356.7 − 45.65
5.	927.0 − 451.7	11.	39 − 32.7
6.	$1,075.34 − $1,008.10	12.	1,000 − 999.99

Answers:

1.	202	7.	944,899
2.	6.3	8.	17.91
3.	7	9.	986
4.	10.91	10.	311.05*
5.	475.3	11.	6.3*
6.	$67.24	12.	0.01*

* add zero(s) to the end of the minuend so that the top and bottom have the same number of digits then subtract.

Once the long method is mastered, a shorter method can be used that involves borrowing within the original problem. Superscripted numbers will represent all the elements of borrowing.

After you've established the phone bill without your line, the boss determines that the size of the phone bill is still too high. "I knew this was the case and I think we should have a little talk with this department to rectify all this." He asks you to find the second highest phone bill and remove it to discover the phone bill with two lines removed. The phone bill with your line removed is $978.89 and the next largest phone bill is $489.92. The problem looks like this:

$$\begin{array}{r} \$978.89 \\ - \ \$489.92 \\ \hline \end{array}$$

The hundredths digit is straightforward: $9 - 2 = 7$, and the difference can be allotted to the hundredths digit.

$$\begin{array}{r} \$978.89 \\ - \ \$489.92 \\ \hline 7 \end{array}$$

The tenths is similar to the last problem in that you need to borrow from the ones to make the tenths adequate. With this example, instead of rewriting the problem, we will use this setup to borrow. It's necessary to borrow 1 one (10 tenths) from the ones for the tenths digit of the total phone bill (minus one phone line). You can memorize the changes so that you can keep your paper clean or you can superscript. I recommend superscripting because even guys with names like Archimedes and Galileo needed to superscript. Superscript 1 to the top left of the eight in the tenths column so that there are now 18 tenths and cross out the 8 in the ones digit of the minuend (top, the total phone bill) and replace it by superscripting 7 above it:

$$
\begin{array}{r}
\$978.89 \\
- \ \$489.92 \\
\hline
7
\end{array}
$$

Subtract 9 from 18 in the tenths digit to result in 9 $(18 - 9 = 9)$ and place the 9 in the tenths digit difference:

$$
\begin{array}{r}
7 \ 1 \\
\$978.89 \\
- \ \$489.92 \\
\hline
97
\end{array}
$$

The same process is repeated in the ones and tens columns because the bottom is greater than the top. The hundreds is straightforward subtraction, resulting in:

$$
\begin{array}{r}
\$978.89 \\
- \ \$489.92 \\
\hline
\mathbf{\$488.97}
\end{array}
$$

Here is a step-by-step demonstration of a subtraction problem with borrowing.

$$
\begin{array}{r}
\text{Example:} \quad \$76{,}345.83 \\
- \ \$69{,}589.79 \\
\hline
\end{array}
$$

----

a.
$$
\begin{array}{r}
7 \\
\$76{,}345.8\cancel{3} \\
- \ \$69{,}589.79 \\
\hline
4
\end{array}
$$

d.
$$
\begin{array}{r}
{}^{2}{}^{13}1\ 7\ 1 \\
\$76{,}\cancel{3}45.\cancel{8}\cancel{3} \\
- \ \$69{,}589.79 \\
\hline
56.04
\end{array}
$$

b.
$$
\begin{array}{r}
7\ 1 \\
\$76{,}345.\cancel{8}\cancel{3} \\
- \ \$69{,}589.79 \\
\hline
04
\end{array}
$$

e.
$$
\begin{array}{r}
5\ {}^{12}{}^{13}1\ 7\ 1 \\
\$7\cancel{6}{,}\cancel{3}45.\cancel{8}\cancel{3} \\
- \ \$69{,}589.79 \\
\hline
756.04
\end{array}
$$

c.
$$
\begin{array}{r}
3\ 1\ 7\ 1 \\
\$76{,}345.\cancel{8}\cancel{3} \\
- \ \$69{,}589.79 \\
\hline
6.04
\end{array}
$$

f.
$$
\begin{array}{r}
6\ {}^{15}{}^{12}{}^{13}1\ 7\ 1 \\
\$\cancel{7}\cancel{6}{,}\cancel{3}45.\cancel{8}\cancel{3} \\
- \ \$69{,}589.79 \\
\hline
\$6{,}756.04
\end{array}
$$

The following are exercises that will help you subtract within the problem. The answers follow.

1.	$3,784 − $ 572		7.	$94,288 − $56,249
2.	$6,089.56 − $3,069.52		8.	$377,295.25 − $ 95,850.89
3.	$45,589 − $38,793		9.	$1,000.26 − $ 955.38
4.	$5,226 − $3,589		10.	$650.37 − $ 2.89
5.	$19,274 − $ 3,683		11.	$14,523.76 − $ 8,718.39
6.	$9,058.56 − $3,297.59		12.	47.04 − 32.089

- -

Answers:

1.	$3,212		7.	$38,039
2.	$3,020.04		8.	$281,444.36
3.	$6,796		9.	$44.88
4.	$1,637		10.	$647.48
5.	$15,591		11.	$5,805.37
6.	$5,760.97		12.	14.951*

* add zero(s) to the end of the minuend so that the top and bottom have the same number of digits, then subtract.

Multiplication

Multiplication is a specific operation of addition that is frequently used. However, it does not mean that multiplication is useless; it's extremely useful and simplifies many problems. Multiplication is an application of addition because it is fast addition. When you add up five 5s, it is not necessary to add repeatedly; you can multiply 5 by 5 instead, giving you the same result as adding.

You may remember how to multiply two numbers, but may have never considered the process you are applying. 5 * 5 is equivalent to 5 + 5 + 5 + 5 + 5. This problem can be completed by adding or multiplying, but multiplying is faster. If the task was to add 378 to itself 50 times, adding becomes a big task, so multiplying is the simpler alternative. 378 * 50 is an application of any simple multiplication and is a lot easier than adding 378 fifty times.

Here are some tips to keep in mind when multiplying:

♦ ( ) ( ) or * or • or x means multiplication. The numbers within the parentheses or around the other symbols represent the numbers to be multiplied.

♦ 3 * 3 means multiply 3 by 3.

♦ 3 * 4 means multiply 3 by 4.

♦ Any number multiplied by 0 equals 0.

♦ 4 * 3 means multiply 4 by 3. It differs from the above only in composition. The answer, 12, is the same, showing that you can multiply numbers in any order.

♦ 2 * 3 * 4 means multiply 2 by 3 and then that product (the result from 2 * 3) by 4.

♦ Any number multiplied by 1 equals that number.

The multiplication table is a basis for multiplication because it shows common products (the answers to multiplication problems). The most commonly used multiplication table involves the numbers 1 through 10 and displays the products of any two numbers from 1 through 10. From this table, any multiplication problem can be employed as an application to the 100 products that are displayed.

It is important that you know how to apply the multiplication table. With it, you will be able to construct and complete more difficult multiplication problems.

The following multiplication table provides answers to the multiplication of any 2 ones digits. The multiplicand (the number that is being multiplied a certain number of times) is found on the left of the table (one of the numbers 1 through 10), while the multiplier (the number of times the multiplicand is being multiplied) is

Table I-1

1	2	3	4	5	6	7	8	9	10
2	4	6	8	10	12	14	16	18	20
3	6	9	12	15	18	21	24	27	30
4	8	12	16	20	24	28	32	36	40
5	10	15	20	25	30	35	40	45	50
6	12	18	24	30	36	42	48	54	60
7	14	21	28	35	42	49	56	63	70
8	16	24	32	40	48	56	64	72	80
9	18	27	36	45	54	63	72	81	90
10	20	30	40	50	60	70	80	90	100

found at the top of the table (one of the numbers 1 through 10). The associated square in which both the row of the multiplicand and the column of the multiplier intersect is the solution.

For example, when multiplying 7 * 8, locate 7 (the multiplicand) in the left hand column of the multiplication table and 8 (the multiplier) in the top row, and follow the row of the 7 and the column of the 8 until they meet. The square in which they meet contains the solution: 56. This is demonstrated in Table I-2.

Table I-2

1	2	3	4	5	6	7	8	9	10
2	4	6	8	10	12	14	16	18	20
3	6	9	12	15	18	21	24	27	30
4	8	12	16	20	24	28	32	36	40
5	10	15	20	25	30	35	40	45	50
6	12	18	24	30	36	42	48	54	60
7	14	21	28	35	42	49	56	63	70
8	16	24	32	40	48	56	64	72	80
9	18	27	36	45	54	63	72	81	90
10	20	30	40	50	60	70	80	90	100

Multiplication of complex numbers (any number with two or more digits) is only an application of this multiplication table. When you multiply two numbers, you multiply every digit of the top by every digit of the bottom. This is a rule that transcends multiplication. The following example will demonstrate why this is mentioned and how every digit of the top is multiplied by every digit of the bottom.

Your boss left you for a while and as you hear the rumble you have associated with his approach, you prepare by looking at the phone bill again. He rounds the corner and—surprise, surprise—asks you about the phone bill. He wants to know what the phone bill would total if every line in the department had the same charges as his line.

Searching through the bill, you find that his line had a charge of $98.56. There are 13 people in the department, each with his or her own phone line. So the problem at hand is to multiply $98.56 by 13 to find the phone bill if everyone was as conscientious as the boss about their phone behavior. To multiply $98.56 by 13, we will apply the multiplication table to develop what are referred to as subproducts. We will multiply the ones digit of the multiplier by the multiplicand, then add that to the second subproduct (the tens digit of the multiplier multiplied by the multiplicand).

$$\begin{array}{r} \$98.56 \\ *13 \\ \hline \end{array}$$

In this problem, we are going to multiply each digit of the bottom by each digit of the top. The way we do this is by creating subproducts from each digit of the bottom. A subproduct is simply a part of the product, and when all subproducts are added together, they become the product. The first subproduct is found by multiplying the ones digit of the multiplier (3) by every digit of the multiplicand. Three is multiplied by 6 to result in 18 hundredths. Because 18 is greater than 9 (18>9), we need to carry the value of 1 ten to the tenths column and allot 8 hundredths to the hundredths:

$$
\begin{array}{r}
1 \\
\$98.56 \\
* \ 13 \\
\hline
8
\end{array}
$$

Then the remaining digits in the top are multiplied by 3 (carrying when necessary) and the first subproduct looks like this:

$$
\begin{array}{r}
2 \ 1 \ 1 \\
\$98.56 \\
* \quad 13 \\
\hline
295 \ 68
\end{array}
$$

The second subproduct is found by multiplying the tens digit of the multiplier (1) by the multiplicand. Remember, any number multiplied by 1 equals that number, so in this case, 9856 * 1 = 9856. But in actuality, we are multiplying 9856 by 10 (because one 10 is in the tens place) so we need to incorporate the fact that we are increasing the magnitude of the subproduct by 10 by adding a 0 in the ones digit of the second subproduct, like this:

$$
\begin{array}{r}
\$98.56 \\
* \quad 13 \\
\hline
295 \ 68 \\
0
\end{array}
$$

And the second subproduct is placed under the first:

$$\begin{array}{r} \$98.56 \\ * \ \ 13 \\ \hline 295\ 68 \\ 985\ 60 \end{array}$$

You will find that you need to increase the magnitude of subproducts often in compound multiplication problems. Increase the magnitude the value of the multiplier, i.e., you multiplied 1 ten by the multiplicand in this last subproduct and increased the magnitude 10 times by adding a 0 to the subproduct ones place. If the multiplier was 313 and another subproduct is needed, the third subproduct would be increased by a magnitude of 100—two 0s would be placed in the third subproduct (taking the places of the hundredths and tenths).

After the subproducts have been created, add them together to obtain a final product. This is why it is important to increase the magnitude of some of the subproducts—so that the appropriate place is kept. Adding the two subproducts gives you:

$$\begin{array}{r} \$98.56 \\ * \ \ 13 \\ \hline 295\ 68 \\ + \ 985\ 60 \\ \hline 1281\ 28 \end{array}$$

The decimal point is placed two digits to the left of the end digit as follows:

$$\begin{array}{r} \$98.56 \\ \underline{*\quad 13} \\ 295\ 68 \\ \underline{+\ 985\ 60} \\ \$1,281.28 \end{array}$$

The decimal is placed there because the original problem contains a total of two numbers to the right of the decimal in both the multiplier and multiplicand. The rule is: If there are decimal points in a multiplication problem, multiply the numbers as normal, ignoring the decimals. Then count the total number of digits to the right of the decimal points in both the multiplier and multiplicand. In the product, start with the end digit (on the right) and count to the left the same number of total digits to the right of the decimal points in both the multiplier and multiplicand and place the decimal point there.

For example, if 5.8997 (with four digits to the right of the decimal point) is to be multiplied by 2.9 (with one digit to the right of the decimal point), the decimal point would be placed five digits to the left of the end of the product. The product of 58,997 and 29 is 1,710,913 and the product of 5.8997 and 2.9 is 17.10913.

The following shows you step-by-step how to create three subproducts and add them together to result in the product.

Example: $143.9
            *   98.4

----

a.
    1 13
    143.9
  *   98.4
    5756

b.
    3 37
    143.9
  *   98.4
    5756
  115120

c.
    338
    143.9
  *   98.4
    5756
  115120
 1295100

d.
    143.9
  *   98.4
  1 1
    5756
  115120
+ 1295100
 1415976

e.
    143.9
  *   98.4
  1 1
    5756
  115120
+ 1295100
$14,159.76

Here are some exercises to update your multiplication skills.

1.	23 * 5		7.	288.25 * 32.4
2.	2.7 * 1.8		8.	5,670.02 * 5.7
3.	56 * 5.6		9.	313 * 79.5
4.	564 * 2.28		10.	1,228.99 * 3.75
5.	329.98 * 45		11.	$437.99 * $500.01
6.	759 * 382		12.	$0.0409 * $0.0022

Answers:

1.	115		7.	9,339.300
2.	4.86		8.	32,319.114
3.	313.6		9.	24,883.5
4.	1,285.92		10.	4,608.7125
5.	14,849.10		11.	$218,999.37
6.	289,938		12.	$0.0000899

Last bit on multiplication

Exponent may be a term you have heard thrown around. An exponent represents the number of times a number is multiplied by itself. It is symbolized as follows:

$$4^3$$

This exponent means that 4 is multiplied by itself 3 times or:

$$4^3 = 4 * 4 * 4 = 64.$$

Division

Learning multiplication also teaches the basics of division, because division is the inverse of multiplication. When asked to divide two numbers, you are also asked the number of times a number is existent in another number. "What is 6 divided by 2?" asks the same question as "How many 2s exist in 6?" There are three 2s in 6 because 3 * 2 = 6. The question and answer can be written in many forms:

$$6/2 = 3 \quad \textbf{or} \quad 6 \div 2 = 3 \quad \textbf{or} \quad 2\overline{)6} = 3 \quad \textbf{or} \quad \frac{6}{2} = 3.$$

Similarly, any division question can be checked by inverting it into a multiplication problem. The inverse of $78 \div 6 = 13$ is $13 * 6 = 78$. So when you are dividing 78 by 6, you may ask, "What number multiplied by 6 will produce the result 78?" The process of complex division will be explained in full by the following example:

With the information that the phone bill would be $1,281.28 if all the phone lines had the same charges, the boss wants to find out how the average cost per phone line compares to the cost of his line. The word average *should instantly signify division because an average entails dividing a number by another to find a normal rate of occurrence. The average cost of the phone lines will result in a number that represents the typical charge for a phone line. The total phone bill is $1,584.76 and the number of lines in the department is 13, so the problem at hand is $1,584.76 ÷ 13 (or "What number multiplied by 13 equals 1,584.76?"). Not many of us know this offhand, so we need to set up and divide using long division:*

$$13\overline{)\$1{,}584.76}$$

First, we should remove dollar signs, commas, decimal points, and any other symbols to eliminate confusion:

$$13\overline{)158476}$$

Then, we divide the divisor (the number to the left, the one that is dividing the dividend) into the digit farthest to the left of the dividend (the dividend is the number to the right, the number that is being divided). The digit we divide first is 1. However, 1 is too small to divide into, so we will carry 1 to the next digit, which, in essence, means that we will try to divide the two digits farthest to the left by the divisor. When we divide a digit (or possibly more than one digit) of the dividend by the divisor and the result does not yield at least 1, we carry the value to the next digit and attempt to multiply the combined digits by the divisor.

So now we try to divide 15 by 13. This is possible because there is a whole 13 contained within 15 (with some extra, or left over). Therefore, we place 1 above the 5 of the dividend and find the amount that remains by multiplying 1 by 13 and subtracting the product from 15, like so:

$$
\begin{array}{r}
1 \\
13\overline{)158476} \\
\underline{13} \\
2
\end{array}
$$

Then we bring down the rest of the digits from the dividend to form a new dividend beginning with the remainder 2.

$$
\begin{array}{r}
1 \\
13\overline{)158476} \\
\underline{13} \\
28476
\end{array}
$$

Divide the next number of the new dividend (the new dividend is 28476) that is divisible by 13. Twenty-eight of the new dividend is divided by 13. There are two 13s in 28 with some remainder, so we place 2 above the 8 of the dividend. Multiply 2 by 13 and subtract that from 28 to find the remainder, 2, while bringing down the rest of the dividend to create the new dividend (2476):

$$
\begin{array}{r}
1219 \\
13\overline{)158476} \\
\underline{13} \\
28476 \\
\underline{26} \\
2476
\end{array}
$$

Dividing the first two numbers of the dividend (24) by 13 results in 1 (because there is a number between 1 and 2 that when multiplied by 13 equals 24). A 1 is placed above 4 of the dividend, then multiplied by 13 and subtracted from 24 to result in the new dividend:

$$
\begin{array}{r}
1219 \\
13\overline{)158476} \\
\underline{13} \\
28476 \\
\underline{26} \\
2476 \\
\underline{13} \\
1176
\end{array}
$$

The new dividend is 1176. Divide 117 by 13. (Skip 11 because 13 does not divide into it at least once.) Thirteen goes into 117 nine times because 9 * 13 = 117. Nine is placed above the 7 of the dividend and then multiplied by 13 and subtracted from 117. Because 13 * 9 = 117, there is no remainder, and the rest of the dividend can be brought down:

$$
\begin{array}{r}
1219 \\
13\overline{)158476} \\
\underline{13} \\
28476 \\
\underline{26} \\
2476 \\
\underline{13} \\
1176 \\
\underline{117} \\
6
\end{array}
$$

The decimal place is now put into the quotient (the quotient is the answer to a problem of division). It was removed from the problem simply to avoid confusion. In the quotient, the decimal is placed directly above the decimal of the dividend. A 0 is added to the new dividend in the thousandths digit. This is because 13 will not divide 6 into a number greater than 1, so the next step is to divide 60 by 13. An additional 0 at the end of the dividend does not change the value or magnitude of the dividend because it is placed to the right of the decimal point and any other digit. 60 divided by 13 equals a number greater than 4, but less than 5 (because there is a number between 4 and 5 which, when multiplied by 13, equals 60). Place 0 above the 6 of the dividend and 4 above the 0 of the dividend, then multiply 4 by 13 and subtract that product from 60 to discover the remainder:

$$
\begin{array}{r}
121.904 \\
13\overline{)1584.7600} \\
\underline{13} \\
28476 \\
\underline{26} \\
2476 \\
\underline{13} \\
1176 \\
\underline{117} \\
60 \\
\underline{52} \\
80
\end{array}
$$

This process could go on and on and does in this example. If there comes a time when the divisor does not divide evenly (that is without remainder) after two digits to the right of the decimal, we can round to the hundredths digit. If the thousandths digit is 4 or less, then we can round down, which means that the hundredths digit remains the same. If the thousandths digit is greater than or equal to 5, we round up, which means that we increase the value of the hundredths digit by 1 hundredth. In the example of finding the average phone bill, we round down because the hundredths digit is valued at 4. The final average, then, is $121.90:

$$
\begin{array}{r}
121.90 \\
13\overline{)1584.7600} \\
\underline{13} \\
28476 \\
\underline{26} \\
2476 \\
\underline{13} \\
1176 \\
\underline{117} \\
60 \\
\underline{52} \\
80
\end{array}
$$

- -

The following examples will help you to hone your division skills.

1.	$3\overline{)6}$	7.	$45\overline{)547}$
2.	$5\overline{)55}$	8.	$7.8\overline{)67}$
3.	$12\overline{)144}$	9.	$1.9\overline{)16.2}$
4.	$23\overline{)1,486}$	10.	$35\overline{)398.7}$
5.	$18\overline{)900}$	11.	$90\overline{)450}$
6.	$34\overline{)42}$	12.	$4.8\overline{)465.6}$

- -

Answers:

1.	2	5.	50	9.	8.53
2.	11	6.	1.24	10.	11.39
3.	12	7.	12.16	11.	5
4.	64.61	8.	8.59	12.	97

In an example where there is a number other than 0 to the right of the decimal point in the divisor, we need to adjust the divisor and the dividend to make the divisor a whole number before dividing. Multiplying both the divisor and the dividend by the same number will not change the quotient, and multiplying both sides by a multiple of 10 (10; 100; 1,000; etc.) will make division easier. In exercise 12, we multiply both by 10 to create a new division problem, which will render the same answer:

$$48\overline{)4656}$$

Fractions, decimals, percents, and ratios

You have already learned a bit about fractions, decimals, percents, and ratios. These are all terms that describe a number as a part of a whole.

A fraction describes two numbers in proportion to one another.

For example: $\dfrac{68}{89}$

In this fraction, 68 is the part and 89 is the whole.

To find the value of a fraction such as the one shown above, you'll need to divide. 68/89 = 0.7640 or ≈ 0.76. (≈ means approximately. 0.7640 was rounded to the hundredths digit.) The decimal value of the above fraction (the value of the fraction as a part of 1) is 0.76, derived by dividing. 68 parts of 89 (the fraction) is equal in value to 0.76 parts of 1. A percent is the part of 100.

Therefore, to find a percent from a decimal, multiply the decimal by 100. The percent of the example is .76 * 100 = 76% or 76 parts of 100.

The following summarizes the methods used to transfer between these relationships:

◆ To find a decimal from a fraction, divide the numerator by the denominator.

◆ To find a percent from a fraction, divide the fraction and multiply by 100 (or move the decimal two places to the right).

◆ To find a fraction from the decimal form, you need to know the original base. In the example, the original base is 89, but this information is usually not available. If the original base is available, you can find the fraction by multiplying the base and the decimal form and arranging that number above the base in fraction form.

◆ To find a percent from a decimal, multiply by 100 (or move the decimal point two places to the right).

◆ To find a fraction from a percent, divide the percent by 100 to determine the decimal, then multiply the decimal by the base (if known) to find the numerator and arrange the numerator above the base.

◆ To find a decimal from a percent, divide by 100 (or move the decimal point two places to the left).

A ratio is similar to a fraction in that it shows the relationship between any two numbers. The ratio form of the fraction 68/89 would be 68:89 and is sometimes divided as a fraction to show the part of one that it represents, 68/89 = 0.76. The ratios analyzed in Chapter 3 are shown as ratios that are divided, therefore taking on the decimal form and displayed as the part of 1.

Find the decimal and percent form of the following fractions.

1.	3/12		7.	6/13
2.	4/16		8.	23/56
3.	6/18		9.	2/15
4.	12/60		10.	3.5/8
5.	30/210		11.	5/2.3
6.	11/88		12.	33/39.9

Answers:

1.	0.25, 25%	7.	0.46, 46%
2.	0.25, 25%	8.	0.41, 41%
3.	0.33, 33%	9.	0.13, 13%
4.	0.20, 20%	10.	0.44, 44%
5.	0.14, 14%	11.	2.17, 217%
6.	0.13, 13%	12.	0.83, 83%

Find the fraction form from the following decimals and percents, given that the base for each is 10.

1.	33%		7.	3.5
2.	16%		8.	67%
3.	0.75		9.	90%
4.	2.13		10.	0.83
5.	1.10		11.	20%
6.	0.10		12.	45%

- -

Answers:

1.	3.3/10		7.	35/10
2.	1.6/10		8.	6.7/10
3.	7.5/10		9.	9/10
4.	21.3/10		10.	8.3/10
5.	11/10		11.	2/10
6.	1/10		12.	4.5/10

Averages

Averages are a principle of statistics and are well-known simply as the mean. The mean is the number that typically represents the sample. Means are often used in business to calculate a representative of a number of samples. It is found by adding the samples together and dividing by the number of samples. For instance, if the sales department has 9 computers, the marketing department has 6, the production department has 9, and the administration department has 12, the mean is found by adding the number of computers in each department:

$$
\begin{array}{r}
9 \\
6 \\
9 \\
+\ 12 \\
\hline
36
\end{array}
$$

and dividing by 4, the total number of departments:

$$36 \div 4 = 9$$

Nine computers per department is the mean.

The mode and median are also forms of averages that are commonly used. The mode is the value found most frequently in the sample. In the above sample, the mode is 9. The median is the value that is in the middle of all the values. It differs from the mean because it does not deal with frequency, but rather with comparative size. The median of the sample {9,6,9,12} is 9, because if put in size order, 9 is found exactly in the middle. The median and mode are often used in analytic functions of business such as market research or any time that frequency needs to be noted. The following exercises will help you to practice averages.

Find the mean, median, and mode in each of the following sample sets.

1. {2, 2, 2, 2, 2}
2. {2, 3, 4, 4, 4, 4}
3. {3, 3, 4, 5, 6, 16, 17}
4. {52, 61, 67, 100, 190}
5. {89, 100, 111, 218, 219}
6. {1, 2, 3, 4, 5, 6, 7, 8, 9, 10}

- -

Answers:

1. 2, 2, 2
2. 3.5, no median, 4
3. 7.71, 5, 3
4. 94, 67, no mode
5. 147.4, 111, no mode
6. 5.5, no median, no mode

Before you proceed to financial reporting...

The math skills that you have learned are basic ones that will enable you to follow and compute everything that will be detailed in the next four chapters. If you feel that a deeper math review will help you to progress in the business world, I recommend the companion book of this series, *Business Math for the Numerically Challenged*. *Business Math* explains in more detail all the topics covered in this chapter with shortcuts and higher-level math along with business applications. Remember, financial statements and analysis are not terribly difficult topics to understand if you apply yourself and learn in a progressive manner, so use this math review whenever you feel you do not follow the math.

Chapter 2

Understanding and Using Financial Statements

Effective managers and small business owners need to have a firm grasp of the basics of financial statements in order to analyze them, draw conclusions, and communicate the firm's performance. There are a variety of financial statements that may be used in analyzing a firm's position or performance. The three most common financial statements are the balance sheet, the income statement, and the cash flow statement.

The three most common statements

The balance sheet (sometimes called the statement of financial position) shows all of the items owned or controlled by the firm, the debts owed by the firm, and the public ownership of the firm. (In most small businesses, public ownership does not exist, therefore this part of the balance sheet exists to portray the investment into the business by the owners.) The balance sheet must (obviously) balance, so that assets (possessions of the firm) equal liabilities (expenses and debts of the firm) plus stockholders' equity (investment by the owners). The owners' claims on the assets of the firm (the stockholders' equity) is found by subtracting liability from assets. The difference between the possessions of the firm and the debts (and expenses) of the firm is the money that has been invested in the firm. The amount of money that is left after expenses are paid is money that is either invested back into the firm or pays the investors (whether private owners, as in the case of a small business, or public owners, who hold shares of stock). The following is a commonly expressed accounting equation:

Assets – Liabilities = Stockholders' Equity

Adding Liabilities to both sides results in:

Assets = Liabilities + Stockholders' Equity

The balance sheet adds all the itemized assets together to result in a sum that is equal to and offsets all itemized debts and expenses plus the money invested in the firm.

The income statement summarizes the firm's operations from its economic activities to tally its profit. It studies buying, producing, selling, and providing services for a particular period of time. An income statement includes all of the revenues that the firm generates and all of the expenses that the firm incurs during its operations. The result—revenues minus expenses—is referred to as "the bottom line" or the firm's net income after taxes.

The **cash flow statement** traces the cash activity of the firm, the cash that moved in and the cash that went out of the firm during the reporting period.

The balance sheet

A typical balance sheet is shown on page 57.

I. Left column—total assets:

A. Current assets:

Current assets are cash and possessions of the firm that will usually be turned into cash in less than one year. Examples of current assets are:

1. Cash on hand: Money that can be accessed immediately.
2. Accounts receivable: Amounts due to the firm from sales made to customers.
3. Inventory: Items in a warehouse or stocked in a store awaiting sale in the ordinary course of operation.

The balance sheet in Table II-1 has the following current assets: cash—$194,900; accounts receivable—$243,600; inventory—$730,800; comprising total current assets of $1,169,300.

B. Fixed assets:

Fixed assets are such things as buildings, machinery, and vehicles used to generate revenue for the business but are not for sale in the normal course of

Table II-1
Balance Sheet for 1997

Current Assets				Current Liabilities		
Cash	$194,900			Accounts Payable	$146,200	
Accounts Receivable	$243,600			Notes Payable	$194,900	
Inventory	$730,800			Other Current Liabilities	$97,400	
Total Current Assets	$1,169,300	$1,169,300		Total Current Liabilities	$438,500	
Fixed Assets				Long-Term Liabilities	$194,900	
Plant, prop, equip	$1,339,750			Total Liabilities	$633,400	
Less Depreciation	$803,850			Stockholders' Equity	$1,071,800	
Net fixed assets	$535,900	$535,900				
				Total Liabilities &		
Total Assets	$1,705,200			Stockholder's Equity	$1,705,200	

business activity. In Table II-1, plant, property, and equipment comprise fixed assets, but fixed assets can be itemized in as much detail as necessary.

Net fixed assets are fixed assets minus their accumulated depreciation. Over time, fixed assets usually decline in usefulness and are reduced in value (depreciated) from their original worth. (Depreciation will be discussed fully in the income statement section.) Net fixed assets in Table II-1 are also referred to as net property and equipment (property, plant, and equipment minus depreciation: $1,339,750 − $803,850, which equals $535,900).

C. Total assets:

Total assets are the sum of current assets and net fixed assets. In Table II-1, $1,169,300 + $535,900 = $1,705,200.

II. Right column—total liabilities and stockholders' equity:

A. Current liabilities:

All forms of debt are claims against the company's assets (the assets of the firm serve as collateral to the debtholders) and the classification as current or long-term depends upon the debt's maturity date in relation to the balance sheet date. Current liabilities are debts that take less than one year from the balance sheet date to pay off. As shown in the balance sheet example, current liabilities are accounts payable, notes payable, and other items totaling current liabilities.

1. Accounts payable—Goods, services, and supplies purchased for use in the business operations that have not yet been paid for. Examples of items purchased on account are raw materials used in the manufacturing of goods for sale and supplies used for the production of goods or services. In the example in Table II-1, accounts payable are $146,200.

2. Notes payable—Short-term obligations, loans, or other obligations payable to a bank or other financial institutions in one year or less. On the balance sheet in Table II-1, notes payable total $194,900.

3. Other current liabilities—Obligations of the firm (such as insurance, unemployment tax, interest payable, sales tax, etc.) that are not classified as accounts payable or notes payable. The balance sheet shows the total of other current liabilities as $97,400.

4. Total current liabilities—The sum of all liabilities payable in less than one year. The example in Table II-1 shows total current liabilities of $438,500.

B. Long-term liabilities:

Long-term liabilities, similar to short-term debt, are claims against the firm's assets. In the example, long-term liabilities amount to $194,900 and take the form of mortgages or bonds that the firm has issued to help finance its current operations, and new acquisitions of property, plant, and equipment.

1. Mortgages are debts secured by specific assets of the firm, where the lending institution issues money to the firm in return for term payments.

2. A bond is a promissory note issued by the firm, unsecured by specific assets, stating a specific maturity date by which the firm needs to repay. Bonds take many forms and have many features. Appendix A defines common types of bonds.

C. Total liabilities:

Total liabilities are the sum of total current liabilities and long-term liabilities: $438,500 + $194,900 = $633,400.

D. Stockholders' equity:

Stockholders' equity represents money the firm owes to its owners (the owners' claim against the assets of the firm). In the example, the stockholders' equity is $1,071,800. It is not a liability because these claims against the assets of the firm by its owners are paid immediately.

For corporations, stockholders' equity represents the fundamental foundation of ownership in the firm and includes common stock, preferred stock, additional paid-in capital, retained earnings, and treasury stock. See Appendix B for definitions of all the parts of the stockholders' equity section.

Total Liabilities and Stockholders' Equity:

Total liabilities and stockholders' equity is the sum of total current liabilities and long-term liabilities plus stockholders' equity: $633,400 + $1,071,800 = $1,705,200.

Claim on income and assets

Small businesses have a simple equity structure. Often, the equity section of the balance sheet consists of owners' profits and retained earnings. Profits can be maintained for each owner to provide separate accounting for his or her respective contributions and consequent profit or withdrawal of equity. In a public corporation, the equity structure is not as simple because the firm needs to tally many owners, each with different stakes in the firm. Some owners may be bondholders and others could be stockholders, all with varying degrees of power and claim. This means that the equity structure is itemized and complex. The following is a summary of who has claims and how the claims vary:

1. **Creditors.** Creditors have first claim on the income and assets of the firm. Those creditors holding bonds have a general claim on the firm's income and assets, but do not have a claim on a specific income or asset of the firm. On the other hand, mortgage holders will be backed by specific assets of the firm pledged as security. If the firm defaults on payments to mortgage holders, the specific asset used to secure the mortgage may be liquidated (turned into cash) to pay off the debt.

Generally, bondholders must receive their interest payments, and the firm must meet any stipulations of the indebtedness (for example, a requirement for the firm to invest) or the firm will be considered in default. In the case of default, the firm may be required to allow bondholders to have a claim on the assets and even possibly a role in the management of the firm. (Creditors usually have no role in the firm's management. They only have an impact on management through the restrictive covenants in the bond indenture clauses or through other credit agreements.)

2. **Preferred stockholders.** Preferred stockholders have a claim on income and assets that is secondary to bondholders but ahead of common stockholders. These stockholders are usually paid a set dividend and any additional dividend payments stipulated in the stock agreement. Typically, preferred stockholders do not have a role in the management of the firm unless there is a violation of the agreement between the two parties.

3. **Common stockholders.** Common stockholders have a claim on income and assets, but only after preferred stockholders and bondholders have staked their claims. Common stockholders hold a risky position because of their third-class status, however, they usually make more money in return on successful investments.

It is important to note that even though preferred stockholders have a claim on income and assets, a firm's failure to make a preferred or common stock dividend payment is not as serious as failing to make a bond interest payment. Generally, preferred stockholders must be paid their dividends before common stockholders are paid theirs, but unlike interest, dividends are not required to be paid.

Summary of the balance sheet

1. The balance sheet must balance. Assets must equal liabilities plus stockholders' equity as shown in the balance sheet in Table II-1.

2. Current assets are cash and other possessions that are typically used up or turned into cash during an accounting period (typically one year) in the regular course of operation.

3. Property, plant, and equipment are not a direct source of cash inflow and are not converted into cash. They are deemed fixed assets separate from current assets.

4. Current liabilities will typically be paid off within one year. Long-term liabilities or debt will remain outstanding longer and will generally not be paid off within a short period of time.

5. Equity in the firm may take many forms: common stock, preferred stock, treasury stock, additional paid-in capital (additional investments by the owners), or retained earnings. Treasury stock is subtracted from total stockholders' equity because it is no longer active stock (there is no claim against the assets of the firm). However, the primary ownership interest of a corporation is through the common stockholders. Common stockholders are also referred to as residual equity holders because they have the last claim on income and assets.

   Retained earnings are profits the firm has recycled into its assets. It is the profit of the firm not distributed as equity. Retained earnings do not exist in the firm as cash and cannot be relied upon when considering cash transactions.

6. The balance sheet is a financial report of the firm only at a particular point in time. Looking at the balance sheet prepared at a different point in time may present a different picture of the firm.

The income statement

The income statement communicates the expenses and profits of a firm over a particular time period.

An important part of the income statement is the concept of accrual accounting, which matches the expenses incurred by the firm with the revenue generated in a particular period of time by depreciating the expenses. The difference between this and the cash method of accounting is that the cash method bills expenses on the income statement at the time of purchase regardless of the purchase's lifetime. The accrual method reduces (depreciates) the value of the purchase gradually over time on the income statement.

For example, when a firm buys an asset, such as a new piece of equipment, that piece of equipment may be used for more than one accounting period. If the equipment is used to generate revenue over a 10-year period, under the accrual method, that piece of equipment would depreciate over the 10 years it is used to generate revenue and the expense is allocated to those 10 years.

With the cash method of accounting, the cost of the equipment would be charged as an expense when it was paid for. In the accrual method, the goal is to make the income statements true to the firm's financial situation. It would be misleading if the firm bought a machine and expensed the entire item in one period but used it over a 10-year period to generate revenues. To avoid this kind of distortion, most firms, as we did here, use the accrual accounting method. The shortcoming of accrual accounting is that although an expense is depreciated, it may have been paid for at its inception of use. This difference will be recorded in the cash flow statement.

A firm prepares an income statement for an accounting period that it can then modify for internal purposes (by itemizing specific expenses, etc.). These statements provide the firm with an in-depth look at certain portions of the income statement. The simplest income statement is that used for external purposes.

Here is a simple income statement for a manufacturing firm:

Table II-2
Income Statement for the Year
Ended December 31, 1997

Sales		$2,436,000
Cost of Goods Sold:		
Materials	$925,500	
Labor	$584,600	
Heat, Light, & Power	$87,700	
Indirect Labor	$146,200	
Depreciation	$53,600	
	$1,797,600	$1,797,600
Gross Margin		$638,400
Operating Expenses:		
Selling Expenses	$243,600	
Administrative Expenses	$280,600	
Total Selling & Administration Expenses:	$524,200	$524,200
Income Before Interest & Taxes		$114,200
Interest Expense		$11,700
Net Income Before Taxes		$102,500
Income Taxes		$40,000
Net Income		$62,500

The income statement shows how every expense account affects the sales of the firm resulting in its net income ("the bottom line") and contains the following parts.

1. *Sales:*

This includes all sales made by the firm during the particular accounting period—1997 in our example. Notice that in this statement there is only one sales amount: $2,436,000. In other financial statements (for example, an internal income statement), it may be important to specify the sales of different products or product lines, along with other figures, to provide a more detailed analysis.

2. *Cost of goods sold:*

Cost of goods sold in this particular income statement includes items that are related to the cost of producing or purchasing the goods that were sold during that accounting period. Production costs consist of materials ($925,500) and labor ($584,600) directly associated with the final product, and manufacturing overhead. Manufacturing overhead is costs associated indirectly with production and includes heat, light, and power ($87,700); indirect labor ($146,200); and the depreciation during that accounting period for the equipment used in producing the goods that were sold ($53,600). Indirect labor refers to labor not directly related to manufacturing the good or service the firm produces, and can include janitors or warehouse staff. The total cost of goods sold in the example is $1,797,600.

3. Gross margin:

Gross margin (net sales) consists of sales minus the costs of goods sold. In this case it is $2,436,000 − $1,797,600 = $638,400. Gross margin represents the mark-up on the goods that have been sold over the cost to produce or acquire the items sold in that period.

4. Operating expenses:

Operating expenses refers to expenses incurred during the selling period that are not directly related to sales. These expenses are associated with a period of time rather than with the product. In our example, operating expenses consist of selling and administrative expenses, totaling $524,200.

A. Selling expenses:

The expenses of selling the product in Table II-2 amounted to $243,600 during the accounting period. Specifically, selling expenses are marketing, sales, marketing and sales salaries, and advertising.

B. Administrative expenses:

Administrative expenses (also referred to as general expenses) of the firm cost $280,600 this period. This includes executive salaries (except the sales force, but usually including the marketing force), clerical help, and all other costs associated with the general administration of the firm's activities.

5. Income before interest and taxes:

Earnings before interest and taxes in the income statement in Table II-2 is $114,200. It is important that this figure exceed its interest and tax payments because the organization must have enough income to meet its interest payments and pay taxes. This is also an important measure of the firm's operations before considering its financial obligations and taxes because it determines the firm's income level.

6. Interest expense:

Interest expense is $11,700 in Table II-2. The expense is interest incurred on all types of debt and is a tax deductible item, which explains why it is listed before taxes are removed.

7. Net income before taxes:

Net income before taxes in the example is $102,500 and reflects revenues from sales minus the cost of goods sold, operating expenses, and interest expenses. Income taxes are then deducted to result in net income. Federal income tax percentage is determined by income level. In our example, federal income tax is 39 percent and 39 percent of $102,500 is $40,000 (approximated). Other taxes, such as state, FICA, and city, may also apply.

8. Net income:

Net income, or what is often referred to as "the bottom line," is net income before taxes minus income taxes: $102,500 − $40,000 = $62,500.

Summary of the income statement

1. Income statements contain the revenues and expenses incurred by a firm in a particular accounting period.

2. Net income arrived at under the accrual accounting method differs from that found with the cash basis because of such items as sales that have been made but not yet collected (accounts receivable), purchases made but not yet paid for (accounts payable), and equipment purchased with cash where the expense is distributed over the life of the asset (depreciation). Net income does not necessarily represent cash.

3. It is important to remember that the interest on debt is a tax deductible expense and should be included on the income statement. Dividend payments made to stockholders are not operations expenses and are not tax deductible. They should not be included in the income statement, but they do represent an outflow of cash.

4. The income statement used for managerial purposes may differ from the one used for tax or external reporting purposes. This is not intended to be misleading, but rather to communicate better the results of the firm to its managers. Internal income statements are more specific because they itemize each account. They do not need to adhere to the strict standards of the Financial Accounting Standards Board (FASB) and differ from firm to firm.

5. The income statement is more than a report card. It not only tells how the firm performed financially but may give some indication of why it performed the way it did.

The cash flow statement

In today's competitive business environment, cash flow analysis has become increasingly important to firms as they have to rely on their internal cash management for business expansion. Cash flow involves determining where cash came from, what it was used for, and the change in cash flow that occurred during an accounting period. Managing cash flow transcends all areas of a business—accounts receivable collection, payments to vendors, timing of purchases and sales of inventory, etc. Monitoring cash flow is also important when planning for the servicing of long-term debt obligations, especially in highly leveraged companies (those that rely on credit to operate). For a new business, not having the cash to make interest and principal payments on loans can lead to bankruptcy.

A cash flow statement measures the cash that comes in (cash inflows) and cash that goes out (cash outflows) of a business. Like the typical income statement, the cash flow statement incorporates depreciation, but unlike the income statement, the cash flow statement is not based on the accrual method.

A typical cash flow statement is shown in Table II-3. (Any number in parentheses is a negative number, representing a decrease in cash.)

Table II-3
Statement of Cash Flow for the
Year Ended December 31, 1997

Cash Flow from Operating Activities:

Net Income (from Table II-2)		$62,500
Add (or deduct) items not affecting cash:		
Depreciation Expense	$53,600	
Decrease in Accounts Receivable	$10,500	
Increase in Accounts Payable	$15,400	
Net Items not Affecting Cash	$79,500	$79,500
Net Cash Flow from Operating Activities		$142,000
(after items not affecting cash)		
Cash Flow from Investing Activities		
Sale of Land	$5,000	
Purchase of Equipment	$(170,000)	
Net Cash used by Investing Activities	$(165,000)	$(165,000)
Net Cash Flow from Operating Activities		$(23,000)
(after items not affecting cash and		
investing activities)		
Cash Flow from Financing Activities		
Payment of Cash Dividends	(50,000)	
Issuance of Bonds	$100,000	
Net Cash Proceeds from Financing Activities	$50,000	$50,000
Net Increase (or decrease) in Cash		$27,000
Beginning Cash Balance		$167,900
Ending Cash Balance		$194,900

In the following activities, the firm's cash is either increasing or decreasing. The goal is to find a net increase or decrease in cash, the cash flow.

1. Cash flow from operating activities:

The cash flow from operating activities converts net income (determined by the accrual method of accounting) to net cash flow by eliminating noncash revenues and noncash expenses (because the statement only concerns cash). For example, the depreciation expense of $53,600 (a noncash expense) must be added back to net income to arrive at net cash flow. Additionally, changes in accrued accounts adjust net income to cash flow.

For example, in Table II-3, accounts receivable decreased $10,500 from the beginning of the year to the end of the year. This $10,500 represents increased cash collections of sales that were "accrued" into income as sales in another period but not collected as cash until the current period. The same is true for the increase in accounts payable.

2. Net items not affecting cash:

The sum of all items not affecting cash. In Table II-3, the sum is $53,600 + $10,500 + $15,400 = $79,500.

3. Net cash flow from operating activities (after items not affecting cash):

Net income added to all items not affecting cash: $62,500 + $79,500 = $142,000.

4. Cash flow from investing activities:

Investing activities are transactions related to assets bought by a company. For example, this company purchased additional equipment for $170,000 to expand production which decreases cash flow in the current period to hopefully increase operating cash flow in the future with added sales volume. The sale of land increases cash flow by $5,000 and the result is net cash used by investing activities: $5,000 – $170,000 = ($165,000).

5. Net cash flow from operating activities (after items not affecting cash and investing activities):

Net income added (or subtracted) to all items not affecting cash results in the net cash flow of $142,000, and subtracting (or adding) the investing activities ($165,000) results in a negative $23,000—($23,000).

6. Cash flow from financing activities:

Any stocks or bonds purchased increases cash flow, by $100,000 in Table II-3. Any payments, such as dividends, decrease cash flow (by $50,000 in the example), resulting in net cash from financing activities of $50,000.

7. Net cash flow from operating activities (after items not affecting cash, investing activities, and financing activities):

Net income added to (or subtracted from) all items not affecting cash minus net cash used for investing activities results in a negative $23,000, and adding (or subtracting) the cash flow to financing activities results in

$27,000. This figure is also known as the net increase (or decrease) in cash.

8. Beginning and ending cash balance:

The bottom portion of the cash flow statement reconciles the cash account from the beginning of the year to the end of the year. This acts as "proof" of the accuracy of the cash-basis adjustments. The ending cash balance should equal the cash balance on the balance sheet and is found by adding the net increase in cash to (or subtracting the net decrease in cash from) the beginning cash balance. In this example, let's suppose the beginning cash balance is $167,900. This is added to the net increase in cash of $27,000, to result in the ending cash balance of $194,900.

Unlike the balance sheet and income statement, the cash flow statement provides a summary of all the cash operating, investing, and financing activities. Examples of transactions that fall into each of the categories of activities are seen in Appendix C.

Summary of the cash flow statement

1. For many analysts of financial information, cash flow provides a better standard to evaluate operating success, liquidity, and financial health because it shows the change in cash during an accounting period. Similarly, a checking account statement shows the change of cash balance during the month.

2. The cash flow statement provides a detailed summary of all of the company's cash activities in operating, investing, and financing for the year.

3. Preparing and analyzing a statement of cash flow requires the use of a comparative balance sheet (showing changes in accounts), a current income statement, and other detailed financial information, such as itemized spending, if necessary.

4. Managers should analyze cash flows as often as other financial statements because it is critical that a company continually monitors its ability to meet operating and credit needs.

Conclusions about financial statements

Financial statements are used for a wide variety of purposes. Investors and managers may want to analyze these statements to judge the productivity, profitability, and future prospects of the business for their own reasons.

The balance sheet and the income statement must be analyzed to determine if the firm is fiscally sound. The cash flow statement must then be analyzed to determine the consistency and stability of the firm. This information provides insight into whether the firm has good management and strong potential.

These financial statements, along with the ratios that will be presented in Chapter 3, and the forecasting techniques in Chapter 4, will provide anyone with the ability to determine a firm's financial condition.

Who uses financial statements?

Individuals or institutions considering making a loan to a firm may take a slightly different view than analysts considering investing in the firm as owners. Present and prospective creditors are concerned with the amount of debt the firm has and the ability of the firm to pay future debts. People interested in taking over a firm also analyze financial statements. This group will be interested in the firm's profit potential, its cash flow potential, and how much additional investment is necessary or what assets need to be sold to pay for the purchase of the firm while still maintaining the primary operations.

But the group who most frequently uses financial statements for analysis is a firm's managers or owners. They have the same concerns as bankers, lending institutions, people taking over the firm, and external financial analysts. They need to know the firm's financial statements in order to provide better management. For managerial purposes, they primarily look at the income statement because it is very much like a report card for the firm. The income statement lets you see how the firm has performed by looking at how, in relation to all expenses, the firm acquired its final profit. The balance sheet, in conjunction with the income statement, determines whether assets have been as productive as they could be. The cash flow statement provides managers with the knowledge of how expenses are handled and how much cash is present during the reporting period.

Analyzing financial data is critical for the owners and managers of a new business. Many entrepreneurs do not have the necessary financial background to analyze statements and completely ignore financial data. This only represents a lack of understanding. Any manager or owner (not just a new business) needs to stay well-informed about the business's financial matters. It is extremely important for small business owners (and, of course, large-firm managers and large-business owners or potential owners) to study their company's financial statements. It can mean the difference between success and failure.

It is important to understand that even though managers, financial analysts, lenders and individuals interested in taking over the business may look at the company from different angles and have different basic concerns, their fundamental analyses will be similar in many ways. They are all interested in determining the success of the firm. Any user of financial statements must clearly understand that financial statements are only one portion of the information used to better understand the firm's operations or enhance its performance.

Chapter 3

Analyzing
Financial
Statements

In this chapter, we address understanding and analyzing financial statements. A strong understanding is necessary in order to make conclusions about what is right or wrong with a firm. Financial statements become more informative when the user analyzes the relationships of particular accounts or groups of accounts in those statements. The information is further enhanced if these analyses are compared over a number of years or to benchmark norms developed from financial statements of a representative sample of several firms in the same industry. This chapter examines the basic techniques of financial statement analysis using ratios and common-size statements.

Ratios are comparisons of one item to another, expressing the size of an item in relation to the other. The ratio of workdays to days off requires that the number of workdays be divided by the number of days off. In a normal week, the ratio of workdays to days off is five divided by two (sometimes referred to as five to two) or 5:2.

This chapter divides 16 of the most commonly used ratios into three groups—liquidity ratios, asset utilization ratios, and profitability ratios—that comprise the main thrust of financial statement analysis.

Liquidity ratios

Liquidity ratios are designed to show how liquid a firm is. They describe a firm's ability to turn assets into cash or the firm's ability to cover current debts with cash reserves and other available assets. The three most common liquidity ratios are the current ratio, the acid-test ratio, and the individual current asset ratio.

Current Ratio: The ratio of current assets to current liabilities.

$$\text{Current Ratio} = \frac{\text{Current Assets}}{\text{Current Liabilities}}$$

The current ratio gives an indication of a firm's ability to pay its current liabilities when they come due. Current assets are resources such as cash, accounts receivable, inventories, and other assets that typically will be turned into cash in less than a year. Current liabilities include accounts payable, notes payable, and other liabilities that will be paid off within a year. The ability to pay these obligations rests largely on a firm's ability to generate cash from current assets, as well as the firm's general profitability. Generally, the current ratio should be larger than one (1). However, the current ratio should be based on industry standards and the firm's experience in the business.

Quick or Acid-Test Ratio: The ratio of current assets, minus inventory, to current liabilities.

$$\text{Acid-Test Ratio} = \frac{\text{Current Assets} - \text{Inventory}}{\text{Current Liabilities}}$$

The acid-test ratio is another check of the firm's liquidity. By subtracting inventory from the current assets, then dividing by the current liabilities, the least liquid asset is removed and it is easier to determine the firm's ability to pay its liabilities using assets that are cash or only one step away from cash. For example, collection of accounts receivable generates cash in only one step. Inventories have not passed the test of being sold and, therefore, are not quite as liquid as other current assets. Expect this ratio to be less than the current ratio in which inventory is an asset.

Individual Current Asset Ratio: The ratio of each individual current asset to total current liabilities.

$$\text{Individual Current Asset Ratio} = \frac{\text{Each Current Asset}}{\text{Current Liabilities}}$$

The individual current asset ratio determines which specific current assets can be used to successfully pay current liabilities by figuring a ratio for each specific asset. For each asset, we will take its account value and divide by the total of current liabilities. The breakdown of the current ratio into individual current asset ratios provides additional help in analyzing the firm's liquidity. It also provides a look at each individual current asset to determine its relationship and liquidity compared to total current liabilities. For example, if the firm can comfortably pay current liabilities when they come due, it has a great deal of cash relative to current liabilities. If the firm has a small amount of cash and a large amount of accounts receivable that may come in after the current liabilities are due, there may be some cause for concern.

If the firm has a large inventory relative to current liabilities and not much cash or accounts receivable, it may be very difficult for the firm to meet its current liabilities as they come due. The inventory must first be sold, and the resulting accounts receivables collected. Each of these two steps requires time.

The current ratio, acid-test ratio, and individual current asset ratios are static measures. Like the balance sheet, each measures the relationship that exists at a particular point in time, not over an accounting period like the balance sheet. While this information is important in assessing the adequacy of existing current assets, it does not reveal anything about when cash will be available as it flows through the accounts.

A question of considerable importance is whether the normal flow of funds from cash to inventory to accounts receivable and back to cash is sufficiently regular and sizable to enable the firm to pay its debts on time. Most current liabilities are incurred during the normal course of acquiring goods and services for the firm's operations.

Inventory acquired this way is converted to accounts receivable when it is sold. Collection of accounts receivable provides the firm with the cash for payment of liabilities. To assess the timing of this process, the average length of time it takes to collect receivables and sell inventory must be computed. Such information measures the activity (and cash flow) within the period's operations, and these calculations are generally referred to as asset utilization, activity ratios, or turnover measures. These activity measures are helpful in judging the efficiency with which the firm uses its current assets.

Asset utilization: activity and turnover ratios

Asset utilization helps determine how effective the firm is in using each of its assets. The ratios involved with asset utilization are referred to as activity ratios or turnover ratios. Activity or turnover ratios show how specific assets are helping the company and the ways liabilities affect the firm. Activity ratios differ from liquidity ratios in that they analyze the actions of selling and collecting. The most common are the inventory turnover ratio, accounts receivable turnover ratio, and average collection period ratio.

Inventory Turnover Ratio: The ratio of sales to average inventory.

$$\text{Inventory Turnover Ratio} = \frac{\text{Sales}}{\text{Avg. Inventory}}$$

The inventory turnover ratio is calculated by dividing sales by the average inventory the firm holds. (While both sales and cost of goods sold can be used in the calculation, they produce different results because sales exceed cost of goods sold by the gross margin.) Most sources providing comparison ratios, such as published industry norms, use sales to compute the inventory turnover ratio. The firm's sales take place over the entire year, while the inventory level is computed at a specific point in time. Therefore, it is necessary to use the average inventory over the accounting period. This is usually done by taking the beginning inventory plus the ending inventory and dividing by two.

Essentially, this ratio attempts to show, relative to average inventory, what kind of sales are being generated. This gives an idea of whether the inventory is too large or too small relative to sales.

Accounts Receivable Turnover Ratio: The ratio of annual credit sales to average accounts receivable.

$$\text{Accounts Receivable Turnover Ratio} = \frac{\text{Annual Credit Sales}}{\text{Average Accounts Receivable}}$$

The accounts receivable turnover ratio explains how efficiently a firm is managing its accounts receivable. If the accounts receivable turnover ratio is too high (credit sales are far greater than accounts receivable), it may indicate that the firm is extending credit terms that are too generous and the firm takes losses on sales never paid for. On the other hand, a firm must offer competitive credit terms or sales will suffer.

Credit sales are used because they generate accounts receivable. As in the computations of the inventory turnover ratio, use averages to avoid distortions that occur when using just one accounts receivable amount at a particular point in time.

Average Collection Period Ratio: The ratio of average accounts receivable to annual credit sales divided by 365.

Average Collection Period Ratio $=$ $\dfrac{\text{Accounts Receivable}}{\text{Annual Credit Sales} / 365}$

Dividing annual credit sales by 365 provides credit sales per day. Then, by dividing accounts receivable by credit sales per day, you arrive at the average length it takes to collect accounts receivable. The average collection period is another important measure in determining how well the firm is managing accounts receivable. If the average collection period is too long (longer than the credit terms), a firm must consider the steps necessary to reduce it or make sure that the credit terms are not too liberal. Be aware that some firms (and texts) divide annual credit sales by 360. This can be considered an acceptable approximation; however, for a more precise result, the more accurate 365 is recommended.

A basic method of evaluating the average collection period ratio is to compare it to the credit terms the firm extends. For example, if the ratio is 45 days and the firm extends credit of 30 days, the firm either has an incorrect credit policy or is not collecting its receivables on a timely basis. If a firm's average collection period is longer than it ought to be, either compared with those of other firms or if it is hampering its profits, and the firm immediately cuts back credit, it may cost the firm dramatically in the amount of sales it makes. There are two sides of the coin in managing accounts receivable: the credit competitors are offering and the kind of credit terms necessary to make sales.

Profitability ratios

By using a number of different accounts, including sales, total assets, and stockholders' equity, profitability ratios give an indication of how effective the firm is in generating profits. There are six ratios in this category, each of which gives a different perspective of profitability. Those most commonly used include the gross profit margin ratio, net profit margin ratio, return on total assets ratio, total asset turnover ratio, fixed asset turnover ratio, and the return on stockholders' equity ratio.

Gross Profit Margin Ratio: The ratio of sales minus cost of goods sold (i.e., materials, labor, manufacturing, overhead) to total sales.

$$\text{Gross Profit Margin Ratio} = \frac{\text{Sales} - \text{Cost of Goods Sold}}{\text{Total Sales}}$$

The gross profit margin ratio indicates how sales are being managed and the cost of goods sold relative to sales. By looking at sales minus only one expense—cost of goods sold—the initial step in determining the firm's profitability is taken. If cost of goods sold (which can be a high-cost item relative to other expenses) cannot be managed, it will greatly reduce the chances of making a high net profit. The gross profit margin ratio is the first step in looking at profitability. Ideally, the gross profit margin ratio should be as close to one (1) as possible because the closer the ratio is to one (1), the smaller is the cost of goods sold. As long as sales are kept up, the cost of goods sold should be kept at a minimum to save money.

Net Profit Margin Ratio: The ratio of net profit to sales.

$$\text{Net Profit Margin Ratio} = \frac{\text{Net Profit}}{\text{Sales}}$$

This ratio can be computed with net profit before or after taxes, but most often, similar to our analysis, it is computed after taxes. This ratio can be found both ways. Depending on circumstances, preferences, and industry standards, a firm needs to determine which way to compute it. This ratio takes out all expenses, then looks at how "the bottom line" net profit compares to sales. Net profit, in many cases, is considered one of the most important aspects of judging a business's success. The ratio of net profit to sales, or the net profit margin, is one of the most critical factors in evaluating how well the firm is performing.

Return on Total Assets Ratio: The ratio of net profit to total assets.

$$\text{Return on Total Assets} \ = \ \frac{\text{Net Profit}}{\text{Total Assets}}$$

This ratio measures the profit the firm earns given its assets and indicates whether it is effectively utilizing total assets to generate profit. This is very important in assessing whether the correct amount and composition of support sales and assets to generate profitability are in place.

Total Asset Turnover Ratio: The ratio of sales to total assets.

$$\text{Total Asset Turnover Ratio} \ = \ \frac{\text{Sales}}{\text{Total Assets}}$$

The total asset turnover ratio indicates the amount of sales that are generated from the firm's assets. This ratio shows how useful assets are in relation to sales. It is extremely important in understanding how productive the firm's assets are in generating sales. If the firm has excess assets, it will appear that it is not generating nearly the sales it should from its total assets. If, in fact, the firm has the correct amount of total assets but not the sales force or sales it should have, the sales area may need to be restructured. This ratio is a useful initial indicator of a problem with sales or an excessive accumulation or scarcity of assets. The analyst, after seeing this ratio as too low or too high, will know to look further into the possibilities of a lack of a sales effort, a declining market for the goods, increased competition, or an improper or inefficient asset base.

Fixed Asset Turnover Ratio: The ratio of sales to fixed assets. (The term "fixed assets" refers to the firm's property, plant, and equipment shown on the balance sheet.)

$$\text{Fixed Asset Turnover} = \frac{\text{Sales}}{\text{Fixed Assets}}$$

The fixed asset turnover ratio, like the total asset turnover ratio, provides information about how successful the firm is in generating sales from its various assets. If this ratio is lower than the firm desires compared to its assets, it means the firm has too many fixed assets or is simply not generating enough sales relative to fixed assets. If it is too high, the firm may have too much invested in fixed assets for the level of sales it generates.

A firm's fixed assets that are not as productive or efficient as those of modern companies may cause the firm to have a much lower fixed asset turnover than the more modern, more productive companies. Currently, U.S. industry places a great deal of emphasis on the productivity of all the firm's assets, including fixed assets.

Return on Stockholders' Equity Ratio: The ratio of net profit to stockholders' equity. (This ratio is also known as the net worth ratio.)

$$\text{Return on Stockholders' Equity Ratio} = \frac{\text{Net Profit}}{\text{Stockholders' Equity}}$$

The return on stockholders' equity ratio indicates what kind of profit is being generated provided the owners' equity. This gives an owner an indication of how productive the business is in generating profits. Owners invest in a business and expect to make a return on their investments. This gives them some indication of how well they are doing. The difference between the return on total assets and the return on stockholders' equity occurs because of a firm's debt.

Leverage ratios

The term "leverage" refers to how much debt a firm has. Leverage ratios compare this debt to other items on the income statement or the balance sheet. It also determines whether interest payments that must be made are covered by current earnings. Leverage ratios are important in determining the likelihood of the firm paying its debt obligations. The more debt a firm has relative to its assets, income producing ability, and equity, the more likely it is to have difficulty meeting those obligations.

Total Debt to Total Assets Ratio: The ratio of total debt to total assets.

Total Debt to Total Assets Ratio $= \dfrac{\text{Total Debt}}{\text{Total Assets}}$

Like with the balance sheet, total assets are equal to total liabilities plus owners' equity. Dividing the total debt by total assets reveals the proportion of total assets financed by total debt. Used in conjunction with profitability ratios, this calculation indicates the degree of difficulty the firm might be in if it has a high debt ratio compared to profit.

Total Debt to Stockholders' Equity Ratio: The ratio of total debt to equity.

Total Debt to Stockholders' Equity Ratio $= \dfrac{\text{Total Debt}}{\text{Stockholders' Equity}}$

This ratio is very important, particularly to those who have invested in the company. Owners of the firm like to know how much total debt there is relative to how much they have invested. A high ratio indicates that the firm may be "highly leveraged" (indebted and subject to default). If a firm is generating substantial earnings on investments (return on assets) that exceed the cost of the debt, then this is a positive position for the common stockholders. On the other hand, if earnings drop, the firm can be in a dangerous position because the cost of liabilities will exceed the amount of profit those liabilities earn.

Times Interest Earned Ratio: The ratio of earnings before interest and taxes to interest charges.

Times
Interest = Earnings Before Interest & Taxes
Earned   Interest Charges
Ratio

The purpose of this ratio is to determine if interest charges are covered by earnings before interest and taxes. It is extremely important that this ratio greatly exceed one (1). If the ratio is one (1) or below, the firm may not be in a position to meet its interest charges. Failure to make interest payments would cause the firm to go into default, which would cause problems with the bondholders.

Ratio computation

Below are examples of the different ratios that have been discussed using information from the income statement and balance sheet in Chapter 2. In the right-hand column are the industry averages, which will be discussed in the analysis phase. (Industry standards and averages are readily available and can be found in many volumes, such as those published by the International Standards Organization (ISO), or on the Internet using keywords such as finance and industry and standards.) The industry averages or standards in Table III-1 are fictional and the type of firm has not been established. In the left column are the sample firm's ratios. (The ratio computations are shown in Appendix I.)

Table III-1
Financial Ratios

Ratio	Firm Ratios	Industry Averages
Current	2.67	2.4
Acid Test	1.00	1.10
Inventory Turnover	3.33X	9.8X
Accounts Receivable Turnover	10X	9X
Average Collection Period	36.5 days	43 days
Gross Profit Margin	26.2%	27.2%
Net Profit Margin	2.57%	3.3%
Return on Assets (ROA)	3.67%	6.6%
Total Asset Turnover	1.43X	2X
Fixed Asset Turnover	4.55X	4.6X
Return on Stockholders' Equity	5.83%	18.1%
Debt/Total Assets	37.1%	63.5%
Debt/Stockholders' Equity	59.1%	174%
Times Interest Earned	9.76X	10.6X

(X indicates times)

1. Strengths:

Current Ratio (current assets/current liabilities)—
The current ratio is high, and it's difficult to determine
whether this is good or bad for the firm. Having debt is
good if it is used wisely, like in the improvement of sales
and profit. However, having debt can be bad if it is not
used for purposeful activities, or if it does not improve

the finances of the firm. As indicated earlier, this figure gives some indication of the company's ability to pay current debt. Upon initial inspection, the current ratio being somewhat high may appear positive. However, additional tests will conclude whether this is true. This will be discussed further in combination with other ratios under the weaknesses section.

Accounts Receivable Turnover (annual credit sales/average accounts receivable)—The accounts receivable turnover is 10 times, as compared to an industry standard of nine times. This, like the average collection period, appears to be good, and it may be. Collecting accounts receivable faster than the industry norm may be beneficial in the very short term, but it could lose a firm sales later because of competitors' generous credit terms, allowing customers to keep their money longer, and making competitors appear more attractive.

Average Collection Period (accounts receivable/ [annual credit sales/365])—The average collection period in the example is 36.5 days while the industry standard is 43 days. Upon first inspection, this also appears to be very positive. However, having an average collection period much shorter than the industry standard can be detrimental as well. In this case, accounts receivable are being collected faster than the industry standard. If this is not hampering sales, then it is positive. It may indicate a better-than-average efficiency in collecting accounts receivable, accuracy in setting policies and stimulating early collection, or it could indicate a far too restrictive collection policy—collecting accounts faster, but possibly losing profitable, although slower-paying, customers.

2. Weaknesses:

Acid-Test Ratio ([current assets – inventory]/current liabilities)—The acid test ratio raises some concern. The industry average of 1.1 percent compared to that of the firm (1 percent) is not much of a concern. But when we look at the firm's current ratio of 2.67 percent, we see a gap between this and the acid-test ratio. Although liabilities may be a possible cause for this gap, upon closer inspection, we see that this can also be caused by the firm's large inventory. This can be determined by taking inventory out of the equation, as we do in the acid-test ratio. By doing this, it also becomes apparent that the firm's inventory is larger than that of other firms in the industry, which indicates that the firm is lacking in liquidity.

This inventory investment will use some cash and the acid-test ratio may fall below the industry standard. This need for cash may be the reason the accounts receivable turnover is faster and the average collection period is shorter than the industry standard.

Gross Profit Margin Ratio (gross margin/total sales) and Net Profit Margin Ratio (net profit/sales)—Both of these figures are below the industry average. This is always a weakness, obviously, because having profits below the industry average indicates that a firm is not earning as much as its competitors. However, the weakness can be blamed on other areas, such as the slow inventory turnover.

Return on Assets (net profit/assets)—The firm is not receiving the profits back from its investment in assets. This can also be blamed on other items, such as debt or delayed receivables.

Inventory Turnover (sales/average inventory)—The inventory turnover at 3.3 percent is extremely low compared to the 9.8 percent industry average. This may be a major concern to the company. The current ratio was high, the acid-test ratio was low, and the inventory turnover is very low. From these three ratios, it can be concluded that large inventories may be a problem. The firm must raise capital to provide assets to operate. If the firm is making excessive investments in inventory, this will cost the firm profits. In this case, the inventory appears to be much too large, which could be a major reason the firm's profits are only about one-third of the industry standard.

Total Asset Turnover (sales/total assets)—Total asset turnover is also below the industry average at 1.43 percent compared to the 2 percent industry standard. This is a result of inventories turning over too slowly and fixed assets not being quite as productive as those of the rest of the industry. As a result, the sales to total assets is far below the industry average and is cause for great concern.

Fixed Asset Turnover (sales/fixed assets)—Fixed asset turnover is also slightly lower than the industry average (4.55 times compared to 4.6 times). This is not enough under the industry average to cause major concern. However, it is not something to be ignored. This indicates that sales are not as high as other firms in the same industry using the same assets.

Return on Stockholders' Equity (net profits/stockholders' equity)—The return that stockholders are receiving on their investments (5.83 percent) is significantly below the industry average (18.1 percent). This weakness results from unproductive assets.

3. Strengths or Weaknesses:

Total Debt to Total Assets (total debt/total assets)—Total debt to total assets is only 37.1 percent compared to 63.5 percent for the industry. Is this good or bad for the firm? Is debt good or bad? Having debt is good if leverage is used as an advantage. It is bad if expenses that are associated with the debt are incurred unnecessarily, which causes a lower profit than desired. Even though debt is very low compared to the industry standard, part of it is being used to finance a very large inventory. While not having much debt could be a plus or a minus for the firm, the inefficient use of it by financing a large inventory is not good management—unless a large inventory is necessary, which makes deviations from the industry standard acceptable.

Total Debt to Stockholders' Equity (total debt/stockholders' equity)—Total debt to stockholders' equity is only 59.1 percent, whereas the industry average is 174 percent. Again, the discussion concerning total debt to stockholders' equity is similar to the discussion of total debt to total assets in that debt is profitable if it is used to the firm's advantage.

Times Interest Earned ([earnings before interest and taxes]/interest charges)—Times interest earned is 9.76 compared to the industry average of 10.6. This is somewhat lower than the industry average, but doesn't raise major concerns at this point. There should be concern if the inventory size suggests that the firm is continuing to manufacture a product it cannot sell. If this is the case, the times interest earned ratio may suddenly worsen.

Common-size analysis

Common-size analysis is another method of analyzing a firm's finances. It removes dollar-size factors out of financial information so that a firm can compare itself to industry averages and standards, as well as to other firms. Common-size analysis shows all the values from the financial statement as the percentage of some whole.

Income Statement—Performing common-size analysis on the income statement consists of dividing all items (except sales) by sales. This provides a "percent of sales" computation. In fact, dividing each item on the income statement by sales expresses each item as a decimal relative to sales. This allows an easy scan of income statements and a look at each item as a percent of sales. Table III-2 shows a sample income statement with percent of sales.

Common-size assessment of the firm

When evaluating the firm's common-size success, the following are strengths and weaknesses compared to other firms in the industry.

Table III-2
The Income Statement with Percent of Sales

			% of Sales	% of Industry Standards
Sales		$2,436,000		
Cost of Goods Sold:				
Materials	$925,500		38.0	37.0
Labor	$584,600		24.0	24.0
Heat, Light & Power	$87,700		3.6	3.5
Indirect Labor	$146,200		6.0	6.0
Depreciation	$53,600			
	$1,797,600	$1,797,600	2.2/73.8	2.3/72.8
Gross Margin		$638,400	26.2	27.2
Operating Expenses:				
Selling Exp.	$243,600		10.0	10.0
Admin. Exp.	$280,600		11.5	10.0
Total Selling & Admin. Expenses	$524,200	$524,200	21.5	20.0
Income Before Interest & Taxes		$114,200	4.7	7.2
Interest Expense		$11,700	0.5	1.0
Net Income Before Taxes		$102,500	4.2	6.2
Federal Income Taxes ($\approx$39%)		$40,000		
Net Income		$62,500	2.6	3.3

Assume that the industry standards given are accurate and appropriate for the income statement.

1. Strengths:

Labor and Indirect Labor—Labor and indirect labor are exactly the same as the industry standards. Labor, as a percentage of sales, is 24 percent for both the firm and the industry standard. Indirect labor, as a percentage of sales, is 56 percent for both. This should be considered a strength because the firm is competitive in the labor market.

Depreciation—At 2.2 percent, depreciation is slightly less than the industry standard (2.3 percent). Because depreciation methods may differ from firm to firm, this is only a slight strength.

2. Weaknesses:

Materials—Materials are costing 38 percent of sales as compared to the industry standard of 37 percent. Although this may seem like a minor deviation, 1 percent on $2,436,000 sales is $24,360 ($0.01 * 2,436,000 = 24,360$). When net income (profit) is $62,500, $24,360 becomes significant because it is almost 40 percent of profits.

Heat, Light, and Power—Heat, light, and power is tallying 3.6 percent of sales, slightly exceeding the industry standard by 0.1 percent. Again, while this seems very small, if this were down to 3.5 percent, it would contribute nearly another $2,500 to profits.

Cost of Goods Sold—Cost of goods sold (73.8 percent) is worse than the industry standard of 72.8 percent as a result of materials and heat, light, and power being worse than the industry standards.

Gross Margin—The gross margin (gross profit) of 26.2 percent is 1 percent lower than the industry standard of 27.2 percent. Given the difficulties with materials and heat, light, and power, this should be expected. While depreciation is slightly less than the industry standard, this can deviate based on depreciation methods, the type of machinery and the quantity of equipment and facilities. Gross margin has clearly suffered primarily because of materials, but also because of heat, light, and power expenses.

Administrative Expenses—Administrative expenses (general expenses) are 1.5 percent higher than they should be relative to industry standards. If general and administrative expenses were reduced to 10 percent and other expenses were held constant, profits would increase by more than $36,000.

Income Before Interest and Taxes—Income before interest and taxes is only 4.7 percent of sales as opposed to the industry standard of 7.2 percent. General and administrative expenses have contributed 1.5 percent to this shortcoming; heat, light, and power contributed a small amount (0.1 percent); and materials contributed 1 percent. Income before interest and taxes is clearly 2.5 percent below industry standards. And 2.5 percent of total sales of $2,436,000 converts to $60,900.

Net Income Before Taxes and Net Income After Taxes—Net profit before taxes and net profit after taxes is much lower than it should be. Because previous expenses exceed industry standards, it is clear why the net profit is 2.6 percent compared to the industry standard of 3.3 percent.

Net Income—As a result of many combined and significant weaknesses, net income (2.6 percent) falls below the industry standard of 3.3 percent.

3. Strength or Weakness:

Selling Expenses—Selling expenses are exactly the same as the industry standard, and this is assumed to be either a strength, or at the very least, not a weakness at this time.

Interest Expense—Interest expense is only half the industry standard. This can be beneficial or damaging depending on how the borrowed money is being used. Interest expense can be profitable if the lender's money is being used wisely and earning a very positive return. On the other hand, having too little interest expense may be detrimental for the firm because it could reduce sales as the result of lost assets. In this case, interest expense falling below the industry standard is not good because profits are well below the industry norms.

Summary of the firm's financial condition

Assuming the industry standards are the correct ones against which to measure the firm's performance, here are some of the difficulties facing this firm.

1. The inventory is too high, causing the current ratio to be too high and the inventory turnover to be far below the industry standards. In part, the inventory ratio accounts for sales to total assets to be substantially below industry standards.

2. A combination of profit squeeze (expenses draining profit) and a low total asset turnover is a result of the inventory being too large, causing the ratio of net profit to total assets to be substantially below the industry average. The combination of expenses and total assets being too high results in the net profit (as a percentage of total assets) being about two-thirds of the industry standard.

3. Materials, as a percentage of sales, are 1 percent higher than industry standards; heat, light, and power are 0.1 percent too high relative to the industry standards; general and administrative expenses are 1.5 percent too high; gross profit of sales is lower than the industry standard; and net profit to sales is lower than the industry standard.

4. Return on equity is far below the industry standard at 5.83 percent compared to 18.1 percent (as seen in Table III-1). The ratios of debt to stockholders' equity and total debt to total assets are far below the industry standards and that has squeezed profit from several areas of the firm. The combination of little debt, high equity, and low net profits have caused the net profit for the common equity holders to be extremely low.

Items such as materials, heat, light, and power, and general and administrative expenses are higher than the industry averages, but they may not be too high given the needs of the firm. It may be that the very tight credit policy has caused sales to be too low. Sales may be causing a great deal of the problem. If sales were higher, all the rest of the ratios may fall into place. Low sales would also force the inventory problem to appear to be very great. Other possibilities that would cause problems with net profit but that may not be apparent in initial analyzation could also apply.

Cautions about ratio analysis

Some appropriate ratios may never be analyzed by others. Do not be bound by the ratios given here or in any other source. If a particular relationship is important to the type of analysis being completed, compute that ratio and develop standards against which to compare it.

Also, when using percentages, you should be careful to not misinterpret results. Percentages can often be misleading if they are not completely understood. For example, if a particular department had an annual turnover rate of 33.3 percent, this may be considered very high until it is revealed that the department had only three people and one of them left. Managers can jump to the wrong conclusions by looking at percentages when they do not understand the underlying numbers. A further caution, as mentioned in Chapter 1, when using percentages: They are not additive (or subtractive, multiplicative, divisible) if their bases are different. Simply adding 20 percent and 40 percent does not necessarily equal a true 60 percent if they are from different basic quantities to start with. In other words, 20 out of 100 (or 20 percent) added to 20 out of 200 (or 10 percent) does not result in 30 percent because the 100 and 200 represent different bases. Forty out of 300 is approximately 13 percent.

Chapter 4

Forecasting

The importance of forecasting is legendary. "If only I had forecasted Snapple or Starbucks" or "I couda avoided that damn stock market crash before the war if only I knew better" are the thoughts of many. In analyzing each industry, we find that particular firms have been more successful and profitable than others. While it may not have been possible to predict what would have taken place within each of these industries, with more precise, intensive planning and forecasting, it might have been possible to alleviate or avoid the downward turn many industries have experienced in the past couple of decades.

This chapter explains how we can use historical financial information to predict—or forecast—changes in business. Overall strategic planning is left for each individual to develop using the forecasting advice contained in this chapter. The purpose here is to introduce the forecasting process as an integral part of strategic planning and explain how it should be used for analysis.

Trend analysis

In Chapter 3, a firm's balance sheet and income statement were analyzed to see why the firm is in its current position. In this chapter, trends will aid this analysis in forecasting the future.

By looking at income statements and balance sheets, trends in the growth rates can be developed. Table IV-1 develops these growth rate trends and shows income statement totals from 1993 to 1997. From these totals, growth trends can be seen progressing. These will be used to develop trends for the last five years with regard to revenues generated from sales and all expenses to operate the business. Why use five years? Why not use six years, 10 years, etc.? There is no magic number. Four or six may be more appropriate, or it may be necessary to use 10. There may be a variety of reasons why statements for more or less years are not appropriate. So it is up to you to choose which works best for you and your situation.

Computing growth rates

To analyze the trends, the information in Table IV-1 is used to compute the growth rates found in Table IV-2. For example, the percent growth rate for sales from 1996 to 1997 is as follows:

$$\text{Percent change in sales from 1996 to 1997} = \frac{1997 \text{ sales} - 1996 \text{ sales}}{1996 \text{ sales}} * 100$$

Table IV-1
Trend Analysis

	1993	1994	1995	1996	1997
Sales	1,679,000	1,847,000	2,031,700	2,219,500	2,436,000
Cost of Goods Sold:					
Materials	655,700	721,300	778,900	849,000	925,500
Labor	425,900	464,200	496,700	534,400	584,600
Heat, Light, & Power	60,500	65,900	71,800	79,000	87,700
Indirect Labor	108,500	115,000	125,400	137,900	146,200
Depreciation	36,600	40,300	44,300	48,700	53,600
Gross Margin	391,800	440,300	514,600	570,500	638,400
Operating Expenses:					
Selling Expenses	161,900	179,800	197,700	217,500	243,600
Administrative Expenses	204,500	220,900	240,700	260,000	280,600
Total Selling & Administrative Expenses	366,400	400,700	438,400	477,500	524,200
Earnings Before Interest and Taxes	25,400	39,600	76,200	93,000	114,200
Interest Expense	8,000	8,800	9,700	10,600	11,700
Net Profit Before Taxes	17,400	30,800	66,500	82,400	102,500
Federal Income Tax (39%)*	6,800	12,000	25,900	32,100	40,000
Net Profit	10,600	18,800	40,600	50,300	62,500

(*Rounded to the nearest hundred)

This equals 10.01% ≈ 10% (≈ is a symbol for approximately equals; 10.01% is approximately equal to 10%). The percentage change for sales between 1993 and 1994 is 10 percent, as shown in Table IV-2.

The general formula used to compute the percentage change in sales from 1993 to 1994, 1994 to 1995, 1995 to 1996, and 1996 to 1997 is:

$$\frac{\text{year's sales} - \text{previous year's sales}}{\text{previous year's sales}} * 100$$

A year's percent change can be applied to expenses, as well.

$$\frac{\text{year's expense} - \text{previous year's expense}}{\text{previous year's expense}} * 100$$

The fifth column of Table IV-2 features the average growth rate for the four growth cycles. The average is calculated by adding the growth rate of each cycle together and then dividing by four. The average percentage change in sales is 9.75 percent, as shown in the average column in Table IV-2. This average is found by adding the results of the change from 1993-94, plus 1994-95, plus 1995-96, plus 1996-97 and dividing by 4.

$$\begin{array}{l}\text{1993-97 Average} \\ \text{\% Sales Increase}\end{array} = \frac{10 + 10 + 9.24 + 9.75}{4} = 9.75$$

Use Appendix E to calculate the remaining growth rates in Table IV-2.

Table IV-2
Growth Rates (in %*)

	93-94	94-95	95-96	96-97	Avg.	Proj.
Sales	10	10	9.24	9.75	9.75	10
Cost of Goods Sold:						
Materials	10	8	9	9	9	9
Labor	9	7	8	9	8.25	8.5
Heat, Light & Power	9	9	10	11	9.75	10
Indirect Labor	6	7	10	6	7.75	8
Depreciation	10	10	10	10	10	10
Selling Expenses	11	10	10	12	10.75	11
Administrative Expenses	8	9	8	8	8.25	8
Interest Expenses	10	10	10	10	10	10

(*Rounded to the nearest whole percent)

Making projections

Now, it's time to make a sales projection based on the percentage growth rates in Table IV-2. From 1993-94, the percentage growth rate is 10 percent, from 1994-95, it is 10 percent, then in 1995-96 it drops to 9.24 percent, and in 1996-97, it is 9.75 percent. The average turns out to be 9.75 percent. The projection is shown as 10 percent. Why not use the average rather than a higher or lower percentage? In every interval, the change was nearly 10 percent, except during 1995-96 when it was 9.24 percent and clearly pulled the average down. The projection is found by adjusting the average slightly upward based on the historical performance. If historical performance showed a downward trend, we would most likely adjust the projection below the average. Again, it is important to remember that this is only an initial projection based on what factors can be seen from previous information, not taking into account a myriad of other factors such as changes in market trends or regional differences in an industry. It should be noted, before predicting the expense growth rates, that it is okay, and even advisable, to overestimate expenses (make conservative estimates) within reason because if a lower expense than the estimate is incurred, the firm will benefit from a surprise of extra income.

The following are the projections for each expense for 1997 based on a breakdown of all expense changes over the past five years, as well the average of each.

The formula for percent increase in an expense between two years is:

$$\frac{\text{year's expense} - \text{previous year's expense}}{\text{previous year's expenses}} * 100$$

Materials—Percentage growth rates for materials have been:

	93-94	94-95	95-96	96-97	Avg.	Proj.
Materials	10	8	9	9	9	9

The initial projection of 9 percent is estimated because materials were only 10 percent one year then 8 percent another year before leveling off at 9 percent in the last two years. Nine percent is the average, as well.

	93-94	94-95	95-96	96-97	Avg.	Proj.
Labor	9	7	8	9	8.25	8.5

Labor is 9 percent in the first and last years of analysis and 7 percent and 8 percent during the interim years. The average is 8.25 percent. Using 8.5 percent is a more conservative estimate than the average for the initial projection. On the costs side, conservative estimates should be a little higher, because if a lower percent actually occurs, the firm will have a surplus of money.

	93-94	94-95	95-96	96-97	Avg.	Proj.
Heat, Light, & Power	9	9	10	11	9.75	11

Heat, light, and power has a 9 percent growth in 1993-94 and 1994-95, 10 percent in 1995-96, and 11 percent in 1996-97. Although the average is 9.75 percent, there has been an upward trend, so at least 11 percent should be used as a growth rate to be conservative.

	93-94	94-95	95-96	96-97	Avg.	Proj.
Indirect Labor	6	7	10	6	7.75	8

Indirect labor has varied a great deal, from 6 percent in the periods 1993-94 and 1996-97 to as high as 10 percent in the 1995-96 period. Even though the average is 7.75 percent, 8 percent would be a better, conservative estimate.

	93-94	94-95	95-96	96-97	Avg.	Proj.
Depreciation	10	10	10	10	10	10

Depreciation remained at 10 percent in all periods so the initial projection should be 10 percent. Note that depreciation, while an expense, is directly related to the amount of equipment purchased and the type of depreciation methods used. Therefore, if more equipment were to be purchased for 1998, depreciation could possibly increase, because there is more equipment to depreciate. The projection then must be altered accordingly.

	93-94	94-95	95-96	96-97	Avg.	Proj.
Selling Expenses	11	10	10	12	10.75	12

Selling expenses are 11 percent in 1993-94 and 10 percent in both 1994-95 and 1995-96, then jump to 12 percent in the 1995-96 interval. The average is 10.75 percent. Because selling expenses grew so much in 1997, use 12 percent for the initial projection. It is extremely conservative and far above the average.

	93-94	94-95	95-96	96-97	Avg.	Proj.
Administrative Expenses	8	9	8	8	8.25	8

Administrative expenses show an 8 percent growth rate in every interval except in 1994-95, where it is 9 percent. The average is 8.25 percent. The initial projection should be 8 percent for increases in administrative expenses because, with one exception, it has been 8 percent the last five years.

Interest	93-94	94-95	95-96	96-97	Avg.	Proj.
Expenses	10	10	10	10	10	10

Interest expenses stayed at 10 percent across the board, so assume that 10 percent is a good projection.

Percent of sales projections

The percent of sales projection is another commonly used approach to forecasting. It uses each expense on the income statement as a percent of total sales to make forecasts. This process is similar to the common-size analysis. The percent of sales forecast serves as a check for other methods of forecasting.

Table IV-3 provides the percent of sales for each expense based on Table IV-1.

Table IV-3
Percent of Sales Forecasts

	1993	1994	1995	1996	1997	Avg.	Proj.
Sales	100	100	100	100	100	100	100
Cost of Goods Sold:							
Materials	39.1	39.1	38.3	38.3	38.0	38.6	38.6
Labor	25.4	25.1	24.4	24.1	24	24.6	24
Heat, Light & Power	3.6	3.6	3.50	3.6	3.6	3.6	3.6
Indirect Labor	6.5	6.2	6.2	6.2	6	6.2	6.2
Depreciation	2.2	2.2	2.2	2.2	2.2	2.2	2.2
Selling Expenses	9.6	9.6	9.7	9.8	10	9.8	10
Administrative Expenses	12.2	11.8	11.9	11.7	11.5	11.8	11.8
Interest Expenses	0.5	0.5	0.5	0.5	0.5	0.5	0.5

To compute your answers, use the partially blank table in Appendix E and the following example:

Materials as a percent of sales for 1997 is:

$$\frac{\text{materials}}{\text{sales}} * 100$$

which equals

$$\frac{\$655,700}{\$1,679,000} * 100$$

which equals

39.1%

The general equation for an expense as the percent of sales is:

$$\frac{\text{expense}}{\text{sales}} * 100$$

Here are two examples of projections based upon the percent of sales:

	1993	1994	1995	1996	1997	Avg.	Proj.
Materials	39.1	39.1	38.3	38.3	38	38.6	38.6

Materials have fluctuated somewhat over time, but the growth percentage increases have been increasing over the past five years, with an average of 38.6 percent. Therefore, a conservative initial estimate for 1998 would be 38.6 percent.

	1993	1994	1995	1996	1997	Avg.	Proj.
Labor	25.4	25.1	24.4	24.1	24	24.6	24

Labor dropped from 25.4 percent in 1993 to 24 percent in 1997. The average is 24.6 percent, but the trend indicates a decline in labor over this period, so 24 percent should be used as a projection.

The projections of all other expenses (with the exception of materials and labor, which are provided above) are provided in Appendix F. This should not limit you to the projections made there. Designing your own projections and reasons for these projections is as important to financial analysis as any expert's opinion. After doing your own projections, compare them to those in Appendix E. Remember, yours may be correct for your situation, more so than the ones provided. If your reasoning is sound and the projection reasonable within the industry, it can be considered appropriate. The broader message is: Based upon information proved, conclude your own results.

The basics of projections have been outlined through analyzing the growth rate and percent of sales. Forecasts can be made based upon this information (as well as other information that may be relevant).

Chapter 5

Developing and Executing a Budget

The next step in financial and overall business planning is to develop a budget, by divisions or departments, based on the financial forecasting explained in Chapter 4 and other relevant information, such as the amount of money allocated to certain departments.

Controlling costs is a difficult task for managers of established enterprises, but is a unique challenge for entrepreneurs who are often so focused on their new products or services that cost control is the last thing on their minds. Lack of a control system is a root cause of why many businesses fail in their infancies.

The budget

A budget is a financial tool that allocates revenues and expenses to divisions or departments. The goal of a budget is to obtain a certain amount of net income from a forecasted volume of sales. Without a budget, it is impossible to know whether the company's actual results are successful or if they fit into the overall business plan.

How to prepare a budget

The budget process begins with the sales forecast because all business activities must rely on the anticipated level of sales. Once a target sales figure has been established, the amount should be given to the head of each budgetary unit (the department): the production manager, the sales manager, the marketing manager, etc.

In smaller businesses, the business owner or the accountant figures the entire budget for the various departments and allows those departments to implement a plan to meet it. However, in a larger organization, the task is too big for one individual, so the managers of the various departments are responsible for preparing their own budgets for approval by upper-level managers. Individual department managers often have more insight into appropriate budgets for their departments. It would obviously be very difficult for the controller of a company to predict the various levels of expenditures needed for each department since he or she usually does not have experience in every area.

Most budgets are prepared for the fiscal or calendar year of the business and usually for each month within that year. Some companies use a "floating" budget, which allows for each department's budget to be reviewed and updated. (For example, the budget begins as January through December, but once January is over, January of the next year is added.) This process keeps budgeting on the minds of managers for the entire year instead of just once a year. Another reason for this method of budgeting is that it is much easier to make changes once new patterns are recognized.

Specific industries may have other approaches to the budgeting process. For instance, a seasonal business, such as a lawn service, may prepare a budget only once for the entire season. Also, certain industries that deal with long-term projects may budget on a contract-by-contract basis in order to determine the profitability of the individual jobs.

Most budgets start out by identifying expenses for which management wants controls established. Thus, departmental budgets are set up for departments such as production, sales, marketing, general and administrative, etc.

Then the individual budget accounts under each of those departments is determined. For example, the production department could include the following:

> Salaries
> Fringe benefits
> Payroll taxes
> Materials
> Utilities
> Repairs and maintenance of equipment

The amount of detail in a budget depends a lot on the sophistication of the company, the necessity of a specified budget, and the amount of time it has spent planning its budgets. The more years a company has budgeted its costs, the more detailed the budgets can be.

This much detail can also be a weakness, because it is extremely difficult to budget individual items of material with any accuracy. There is a fine line between too little and too much detail for an accurate budget. It takes practice to develop the right budget for a particular business. For instance, if all advertising costs are lumped together in a department's budget, it is difficult to tell whether print media advertising or the additional salary expense of a new graphic artist caused a budget overrun.

Here is an example of a typical budget:

Table V-1
Departmental Budget through
December 31, 1998

Sales	$2,700,000
Production Budget	1,800,000
Shipping Budget	100,000
Marketing Budget	300,000
Administrative Budget	200,000
Net Income	300,000

This summarized budget provides the total funds to be allocated to each of the departments of the organization. Sales are anticipated sales and each department's budget is noted to generate a net income goal of $300,000 for the firm. Then each of the department managers determines how to spend his or her allocated funds to most efficiently and effectively establish the targeted sales forecast of $2,700,000.

The following is an example of the detailed budget for the administrative department.

Table V-2
Administrative Budget through
December 31, 1998

Personnel Recruiting Expense	$40,000
Accounting	60,000
Security	15,000
Supplies	35,000
Office Equipment	20,000
Interest Expense	30,000
Total General & Administrative Expenses	200,000

Key facts to remember about the budget

♦ The budgeting process takes a lot of practice. Once implemented and used properly, it is a valuable tool to control costs and increase the profitability of a company.

♦ A budget process must continuously be updated for changes in the company's business environment. An outdated budget does not provide useful information. There is a big advantage in the "floating" budget process, which requires budgeters to constantly update it for changing market conditions, such as increased prices for raw materials or cutbacks in the sales force as the year progresses.

♦ A budget can be as detailed or as summarized as management sees fit as long as it is still useful, especially to the individual with the overall budget responsibilities. If a simple budget, such as the examples in Tables V-1 and V-2, is sufficient, there is no reason to complicate the process and itemize every expense. Simple budgets also allow for flexibility. Does the budget give the owner or CEO of the company all the information necessary to analyze the progress of the entire business as well as the individual departments?

Benefits of the budget

♦ A budget allows for coordination of all the departments of a company. For example, if the company forecasts sales of $10 million, the production department must be allocated sufficient funds to produce enough goods to meet such a goal. The same theory must hold true of all departments in the organization.

♦ A budget is a report that provides managers or small business owners a starting point for taking action to control costs and to correct practices that are causing cost overruns. For example, if the chief executive officer notices that actual entertainment expenses for the sales department were $8,000 and the budget was $3,500, he or she can take whatever action he or she deems appropriate.

♦ A budget develops a standard by which to measure the performance of department managers. In many businesses, "meeting the budget" is the only standard by which to evaluate managers.

That's it!

And there it is—the basics to business finance. With the information you have learned in these few chapters, you can now evaluate a company's financial standings, analyze its position, and anticipate where the company will be going in the next few years. This knowledge will also aid you in making the right decisions for your own company based on properly prepared budgets and financial statements.

Appendix A

Common Bonds

Callable bonds—Bonds with a provision that allows the firm to repurchase them at a specific price at a specific time and retire them before their maturity date.

Convertible bonds—Bonds that may, under certain conditions, be converted into common stock at the bondholder's request. Typically, convertible bonds are issued by firms whose stock prices are low, but whose management expects growth in the stock prices over time, making them attractive for bondholders to convert into stock. This is a convenient way for firms to grow, first using convertible bonds, then growing so that stock prices increase and bondholders convert to common stockholders.

Debenture bonds—Bonds not secured by specific assets of the firm. Like other unsecured debt, debenture bonds are protected, in the firm's view, by assets not specifically pledged to other debtholders.

Sinking fund—A secure fund into which periodic cash deposits are made from bonds that incorporate a provision requiring rush deposits. This cash is then used to pay the bondholder at the bond's maturity date.

Subordinated debentures—Debenture bonds that are secondary to other bonds in their claims on the firm's assets and income.

Appendix B

Elements of Stockholders' Equity

Common stock—Stocks held by a firm's residual and primary owners. The money they make is what is left over after employees are compensated, expenses are paid, etc. Because common stockholders have a residual position, they are the primary risk-takers and have the greatest role in the firm's management. Common stockholders elect the board of directors, who select the management of the firm. Although common stockholders often receive dividends (payments made to stockholders), it is not a requirement for them to be paid. As a result of their risky positions, common stockholders expect higher returns on their investment than either bondholders or preferred stockholders.

Preferred stock—Stock issued by the firm that has preference over common stock. Preferred stock claims income earned and assets before common stock and typically has a stated dividend payment (percentage or dollar amount). Preferred stockholders, however, are not the firm's primary shareholders as more common stock is available for sale, thus making common stockholders the primary owners.

Additional paid-in capital—Amounts paid or invested (in excess of stated values of the common or preferred stock) by the stockholders into the firm.

Treasury stock—Stock issued by the firm, then re-acquired without a provision, but not formally retired by the firm. Its cost is subtracted from the total of all other stockholders' equity items because it does not represent an investment into the firm by the owners.

Retained earnings—Accumulated earnings less dividend distributions that the firm has distributed throughout the assets of the firm. Many dollars of retained earnings are not held in the form of cash, and it is a common misunderstanding that retained earnings are available as cash for the firm to spend. It is a balancing factor in the financial statement as earnings are distributed into assets.

Appendix C

Cash Flow Categories

The following list outlines cash operations that will affect the cash flow statement. The list is categorized into operating, investing, and financing activities, and within each are the items that affect cash inflows and outflows.

Operating activities:

Cash inflows:

1. From sales of goods or services.
2. From returns on investments (interest on loans or dividends on securities).

Cash outflows:

1. To vendors for inventory.
2. To employees for labor.
3. To banks for interest on loans.

Investing activities:

Cash inflows:

1. From sale of fixed assets (property, plant and equipment).
2. From collection of loan to other parties.

Cash outflows:

1. To purchase fixed assets.
2. To make loans to other parties.

Financing activities:

Cash inflows:

1. From issuance of bonds.
2. From sale of capital stock.

Cash outflows:

1. To shareholders as dividends.
2. To redeem bondholders.

As you can see from these sample transactions, there is a pattern to determining where a transaction should be categorized on a statement of cash flows. Operating activities include all transactions that do not fall into the other categories. It generally includes income statement items that have been adjusted to arrive at a cash-basis income. Investing activities typically relate to changes in long-term assets (such as fixed assets), and financing activities include cash flows from changes in long-term debt and equity items on the balance sheet.

Appendix D

Computation of Financial Ratios

Following are computations of financial ratios. All sales, expenses, liabilities, assets, and equity are taken from Tables II-1 and II-2.

Ratio	Equation	Computation	Result
Current	$\dfrac{\text{Current Assets}}{\text{Current Liabilities}}$	$\dfrac{1,169,300}{438,500}$	2.67
Acid Test	$\dfrac{\text{Current Assets} - \text{Inventory}}{\text{Current Liabilities}}$	$\dfrac{1,169,300 - 730,800}{438,500}$	1.00
Inventory Turnover	$\dfrac{\text{Sales}}{\text{Average Inventory}}$	$\dfrac{2,436,000}{730,800}$	3.33 X
Accounts Receivable Turnover	$\dfrac{\text{Annual Credit Sales}}{\text{Avg. Accounts Receivable}}$	$\dfrac{2,436,000}{243,600}$	10 X
Avg. Collection Period	$\dfrac{\text{Accounts Receivable}}{\text{Annual Credit Sales} / 365}$	$\dfrac{243,600}{2,436,000/365}$	36.5 days

Ratio	Equation	Computation	Result
Gross Profit Margin Ratio	Gross Margin / Total Sales	638,400 / 2,436,000	26.2%
Net Profit Margin	Net Profit / Sales	62,500 / 2,436,000	2.57%
Return on Assets (ROA)	Net Profit / Assets	62,500 / 1,705,200	3.67%
Total Asset Turnover	Sales / Assets	2,436,000 / 1,705,200	1.43 X
Fixed Asset Turnover	Sales / Net Fixed Assets	2,436,000 / 535,900	4.55 X
Return on Stockholders' Equity	Net Profits / Stockholders' Equity	62,500 / 1,071,800	5.83%
Debt to Total Assets	Debt / Total Assets	633,400 / 1,705,200	37.1%
Debt to Stockholders' Equity	Total Debt / Stockholders' Equity	633,400 / 1,071,800	59.1%
Times Interest Earned	Earnings Before Int. & Taxes / Interest Charges	114,200 / 11,700	9.76 X

Appendix E

Percent of Sales Forecasts

The following percent of sales forecast table is a partially completed version of Table IV-2. Use this chart to determine the growth rates of sales and expenses accounts using information from Table IV-1 and the explanation on page 111.

	93-94	94-95	95-96	96-97	Avg.	Proj.
Sales	10	10	9.24	9.75	9.75	10
Cost of Goods Sold:						
Materials		8			9	9
Labor	9	7	8		8.25	8.5
Heat, Light & Power				11	9.75	10
Indirect Labor	6	7			7.75	8
Depreciation	10	10	10			10
Selling Expenses	11	10	10			11
Administrative Expenses	8		8	8		
Interest Expenses			10	10	10	

Expenses As a Percent of Sales

The following table is a partially completed version of Table IV-3. Use the data in Table IV-1 and the example on page 117 to complete this table.

	1993	1994	1995	1996	1997	Avg.	Proj.
Sales	100	100	100	100	100	100	100
Cost of Goods Sold:							
Materials	39.1		38.3			38.6	38.6
Labor	25.4			24.1	24	24.6	24
Heat, Light & Power	3.6	3.6				3.6	3.6
Indirect Labor	6.5	6.2	6.2	6.2	6.0		6.2
Depreciation	2.2	2.2	2.2				2.2
Selling Expenses				9.8		9.8	10
Administrative Expenses	12.2	11.8	11.9	11.7			11.8
Interest Expenses			0.5		0.5		

Glossary

Accounts payable—Goods, services, and supplies purchased for business operations, but have not yet been paid for.

Accounts receivable—Amounts that are due the firm from sales made to customers.

Accounts receivable turnover—An activity ratio found by dividing annual credit sales by average accounts receivable.

Accrual accounting—Accounting method that matches expenses incurred by the firm during a certain time period with the revenue generated during the same time period.

Acid-test ratio—A liquidity ratio that measures a firm's ability to pay its liabilities using cash or assets that are only one step away from cash. The ratio is found by subtracting inventory from current assets, then dividing by current liabilities.

Activity ratios (asset utilization or turnover ratios)—Ratios that determine how effective a firm is in utilizing its assets in the management of the firm.

Additional paid-in capital—Investments made into the firm by its stockholders in excess of stated stock values. This does not represent a profit to the firm, but is a component of stockholders' equity.

Asset utilization ratios (activity ratios or turnover ratios)—Ratios that determine how effective a firm is in utilizing its assets in the management of the firm.

Assets—Properties and belongings or other economic resources of a firm that fund operations of the firm and produce profits.

Average collection period ratio—An activity ratio that provides the length of time it takes to collect accounts receivable. The ratio is found by dividing average accounts receivable by annual credit sales, which have been divided by 365.

Balance sheet—Financial report that shows the financial position of a firm at a particular point in time. It lists all the firm's assets and liabilities, as well as the stockholders' (owners') equity.

Bonds—Long-term debt issued by a firm that is used to finance operations. The firm agrees to pay the bondholders periodic interest payments and the face value of the bond at a maturity date, both specified on the bond.

Callable bonds—Bonds with a provision that allows the firm to buy them back before the scheduled maturity date. In the case of a prematurely repurchased bond, the bondholders are usually compensated with a payment higher than the face value of the bond.

Cash flow statement—Report that shows the cash that comes in (cash inflow) or leaves (cash outflow) a firm.

Common equity—Claims against the assets of a business by its owners. It represents the owners' investment in the firm's assets.

Common stock—Stock held by a firm's residual and primary owners. The dividends are paid after employees are compensated, expenses paid, and preferred stock dividends are paid.

Common-size analysis—Percentage comparison and examination of a firm to the industry.

Convertible bonds—Bonds that may, under certain conditions, be converted into common stock.

Cost of goods sold—The total of all items that are directly related to production of goods for sale.

Current ratio—A liquidity ratio that determines a firm's ability to pay its current liabilities. The ratio is found by dividing current assets by current liabilities.

Debenture bonds—Bonds not secured by specific assets of the firm.

Debt to net worth ratio—A ratio that measures amount of debt a firm has compared to the amount of equity that has been invested. This ratio is found by dividing the firm's total debt by its stockholders' equity.

Depreciation—The allocation of the cost of an asset over the accounting periods during which the asset was used.

Equity—The total investment in the firm by outside sources. Equity includes common stock, preferred stock, additional paid-in capital, retained earnings, and treasury stock.

Financial Accounting Standards Board (FASB)—A group, consisting of private sector accounting professionals, important in establishing the generally accepted accounting principles.

Fixed asset turnover ratio—Profitability ratio that measures the success of sales from a firm's fixed assets. This is found by dividing sales by fixed assets.

Fixed assets (property, plant, and equipment)—Assets not for sale during the normal course of business activity, used to generate revenue for the business.

Floating budget—Budget that is constantly reviewed and updated, thus keeping budgeting in the minds of the decision-makers throughout the year, instead of the one time when the annual budget is normally prepared. This process also allows for the changing market conditions, such as increased expenses for materials or cutbacks in the sales force.

Gross margin—Sales minus the cost of goods sold.

Gross profit margin ratio—A profitability ratio that indicates how the cost of goods sold are being managed compared to sales. The ratio is found by dividing sales minus cost of goods sold by total sales.

Income statement—Financial reports that indicate profits as the result of sales revenue minus expenses.

Indenture—The agreement between a firm and its bondholders and stockholders that includes all of the features and restrictive covenants.

Individual current asset ratio—Activity ratio that shows what percent of liabilities are financed by a particular asset. It is found by dividing an individual current asset by total current liabilities.

Inventory turnover ratio—An activity ratio that reveals the size of inventory relative to sales. It is calculated by dividing either sales or cost of goods sold by the firm's average inventory.

Leverage ratios—Ratios that compare the debt of a firm to its holdings.

Liabilities—Short-term and long-term debts of a firm.

Liquidity ratios—Ratios that indicate the case at which a firm can convert its assets to cash. They describe a firm's ability to turn assets into cash or its ability to cover current debts with cash reserves and other available assets.

Net fixed assets—Fixed assets minus their accumulated depreciation.

Net profit margin ratio—Profitability ratio that shows how well a firm is controlling expenses. The ratio is found by dividing net profit (before or after taxes) by sales.

Notes payable—Short-term obligations, usually to a bank rather than another financial institutions, that are payable in one year or less.

Operating expenses—Money spent indirectly for the purpose of generating sales, including selling and administrating expenses.

Percent of sales projection—A commonly employed approach to forecasting that uses each expense on the income statement as a percent of total sales. The percent of sales projection serves as a check for other methods of forecasting.

Preferred stock—Stock that has superiority over common stock with respect to dividends and assets in the case of liquidation.

Profitability ratios—Ratios that mark how effective the firm is at generating profits compared with other entities, such as sales and assets.

Quick-test ratio (acid-test ratio)—Ratio that measures a firm's ability to pay its liabilities using cash or assets that are only one step away from cash. It is found by subtracting inventory from current assets, then dividing by current liabilities.

Retained earnings—The profit of a firm not distributed as equity. Retained earnings do not exist in the firm as cash and cannot be relied upon when considering cash transactions, but rather are a component of stockholders' equity.

Return on stockholders' equity ratio (net worth ratio)—Indicates how much profit has been generated given a specific component of owners' (stockholders') equity. It is computed by dividing net profit by stockholders' equity.

Return on total assets ratio—A profitability ratio computed by dividing the net profit by total assets. This ratio indicates whether a firm is effectively using its total assets to generate profit.

Revenues—Amounts charged to a firm's customers for goods and services received during a particular accounting period.

Sinking fund—A bond with a securing provision that the firm must make payments into an account used to retire a bond.

Stockholders' equity—The total investment in the firm by outside sources. Equity includes common stock, preferred stock, additional paid-in capital, retained earnings, and treasury stock.

Subordinated debenture—Unsecured bonds that are secondary in their claim on the firm's assets and income to other bonds.

Times interest earned ratio—A leverage ratio that shows the percentage of interest that is earned before interest payments and taxes are paid. It is calculated by dividing earnings before interest and taxes by interest charges.

Total asset turnover—Profitability ratio found by dividing sales by total assets. This ratio denotes sales generated by assets.

Total debt to stockholders' equity—Leverage ratio that reveals the percentages of equity that finance debt. It is found by dividing total debt by stockholders' equity.

Total debt to total assets ratio—Average ratio that measures the proportion of total assets that are financed by debt. The ratio is found by dividing total debt by total assets.

Treasury stock—Shares of a firm's stock that have been issued and then reacquired by the firm, but have not yet been formally retired.

Turnover ratios (asset utilization or activity ratios)— Ratios that determine how effective a firm is in utilizing its assets in the management of the firm.

Index

A

Accounting, 64-65, 73
  accrual method, 64, 73, 139
  cash method, 65
Accounts payable, 57-59, 139
Accounts receivable, 56-57, 139
  turnover ratio, 85-86, 95, 139
Accrual accounting, 64, 73, 139
Acid-test ratio, 82-83, 96, 139, 145
Activity ratios, 84-87, 139
Addition, 15-19, 29
Additional paid-in capital, 129, 139
Administrative expenses, 68, 102, 115
Asset utilization, 84-87, 140
Assets, 54-58, 140
Average collection period ratio, 86-87, 95-96, 140
Averages, 49-51

B

Balance sheet, 54-64, 140
Base-ten system, 21
Bonds, 60, 127, 140
Borrowing, 22-23, 27
"Bottom line," 55, 67
Budget, developing and executing, 119-126
Business Math for the Numerically Challenged, 51

C

Callable bonds, 127, 141
Cash flow categories, 131-132
Cash flow statement, 56, 71-76, 141
Cash method of accounting, 65
Cash on hand, 56
Claims on income and assets, 61-63